World Directors Series

Film retains its capacity to beguile, entertain and open up windows onto other cultures like no other medium. Nurtured by the growth of film festivals worldwide and by cinephiles from all continents, a new generation of directors has emerged in this environment over the last few decades.

This new series aims to present and discuss the work of the leading directors from across the world on whom little has been written and whose exciting work merits discussion in an increasingly globalised film culture. Many of these directors have proved to be ambassadors for their national film cultures as well as critics of the societies they represent, dramatising in their work the dilemmas of art that are both national and international, of local relevance and universal appeal.

Written by leading film critics and scholars, each book contains an analysis of the director's works, filmography, bibliography and illustrations. The series will feature film-makers from all continents (including North America), assessing their impact on the art form and their contribution to film culture.

Other Titles in the Series

Youssef Chahine

Forthcoming:
Lars von Trier
Yash Chopra
Emir Kusturica
Terrence Malick

WORLD DIRECTORS

JANE CAMPION

Dana Polan

For my nieces, Kelly, Leigh, Kyra and Moira, and their creative worlds

First published in 2001 by the
BRITISH FILM INSTITUTE
21 Stephen Street, London W1T 1LN

The British Film Institute promotes greater understanding and
appreciation of, and access to, film and moving image culture in the UK.

Cover design: Ketchup
Set by Alden Bookset, Somerset
Printed in England by The Cromwell Press, Trowbridge, Wiltshire

British Library Cataloguing-in-Publication Data
A catalogue record for this book is available from the British Library

ISBN 0–85170–856–0 (pbk)
ISBN 0–85170–857–9 (hbk)

CONTENTS

ACKNOWLEDGMENTS

My gratitude goes to my graduate research assistants Brody Fox and Jared Smith; to my judicious and patient editor Andrew Lockett; to Ella Taylor for support and for rich conversation about Jane Campion; to Sherry Millner and William Caplan for energetic encouragement; to Erinna Mettler of the British Film Institute for assistance on box-office figures. I offer special thanks to friends from Australian film circles who provided me with useful information and research material – Adrian Martin, Noel King, Lesley Stern, Deb Verhoeven, Toby Miller, Laleen Jayamanne, Kate Raynor and Philip Bell – and to Liz Sisco, Doug Stewart and my new friends from New Zealand who met with me over a lovely dinner to talk about growing up in that country – Jean Stewart, Sara Stewart, Doug and Betty Miller.

To Marita Sturken, I offer, as always, my love, deep admiration and appreciation.

One
Resonant Melodies

The Iron Chef, a Japanese cooking show that has acquired a cult following on cable TV for its kitschy mix of samurai style and culinary intrigue, is a quintessential spectacle of machismo. Bedecked in samurai costumes, standing erect and brandishing their kitchen tools as if they were the fetish objects of an elite Ronin clan, the 'Iron Chefs' face 'Challengers' in the gladiator-style 'Kitchen Stadium', engaging in man-to-man combat over the 'secret' ingredient with which they have one hour to prepare a five-course meal for a panel of judges. Throughout, they are accompanied by the trappings of culinary manhood – knives wielded like swords, deferential sous-chefs and underlings, and, in particular, the swelling of imperial, martial music (lots of brass and percussion, with big crescendos). It's a macho extravaganza complete with excessive physicality (the utensils that swoop through the air to chop up fish and fowl), surly sweatiness, taunt, bravado and braggadocio.

Yet, an episode broadcast in May 2000 marked a departure from the exclusively masculine domain of Kitchen Stadium when a young woman chef came as the Challenger, necessitating a means to represent her difference from the male chefs within the highly stylised production. At first, the show tried to contain the difference of femininity by treating the woman's presence as not so different at all: initially, there was the same military music, the same fever-pitch narration that renders the competition as a veritable sports event of talented Titans in battle. But as the narrator began to discuss the personal triumphs and tragedies that the chef had faced and surmounted – especially a traumatic divorce – the music turned in abrupt fashion from military aggressiveness to none other than the lush romantic strains of the Michael Nyman soundtrack for Jane Campion's *The Piano*.

What strikes me about this dramatic shift into the register of the personal and, in particular, of personally felt emotional trauma is the matter-of-fact telegraphic directness of the reference to *The Piano*. The film's soundtrack is assumed to easily, automatically, inevitably and logically connote the realm of the feminine personal, a space of romance sparked and thwarted, a site in which emotional life asserts its irreducible importance even against the demands of a masculinised and professionalised world. The music so associated with *The Piano* becomes here a veritable fixed signifier of affect, emotion and inner value – all associated intimately with the particularity of being a woman. (Is it by accident that the videotape version of *The Piano* available in the USA begins with an advertisement for a free-phone number from which to order flowers and floral arrangements, set to the luxuriant music of Vivaldi?)

The Piano is now a major point of reference for our contemporaneity, an imposing artistic production that for many people encapsulates, for better or for worse, a stylistic and thematic impression of feminine feeling. The exemplary nature of *The Piano* as a condensation of the parameters of such a cultural representation allows it easily to lend itself to stereotyping, as its citation in *The Iron Chef* signals. It can lead as well to parody. For example, the TV show *Saturday Night Live* did a sketch called 'The Washing Machine' with a Holly Hunter look-alike caught in romantic mystery while her daughter cartwheels around her on the surf-swept beach in front of a large white washer. Similarly, *All Men are Liars*, the first feature film by Campion's former boyfriend and collaborator Gerard Lee, begins by chronicling how a piano taken away from a woman by her husband is smashed to smithereens in a highway accident while in transit! In a joint interview, Lee and the film's producer, John Maynard (who has also produced some Jane Campion films), make explicit that this opening intends a direct jocular reference to *The Piano*. For Maynard, 'We thought that opening a film with a woman who doesn't speak playing a piano – already a proven success – would be a good way to start an Australian movie.' And Lee is even more explicit about a need to demarcate himself from Campion: 'We're great friends with Jane and there's nothing personal in it, but I suppose it is taking the piss out of auteur film-making.'[1]

Even more striking in its appropriation of motifs from *The Piano* as re-useable figures of romantic exoticism for directly commercial purposes is a television advertisement starring Anna Paquin (who plays the young daughter Flora in the film), produced the same year as *The Piano* for media giant MCI's Internet network services. To exotic indigenous music, Paquin dances lyrically in silhouette before a setting sun; then in close-up before a bonfire she extols in an awe-struck voice the virtues of new global communication: 'A brain inside a head in Ohio is studied by a surgeon in Tokyo. A mother's face in France appears on a telephone in New York. A virtual journey to any moment in time. The possibilities are endless.' As the last phrases are uttered, there is a quick shot to what seems to be an American Indian in tribal outfit and then an image of Paquin dancing on a beach in ways that directly approximate early shots from *The Piano*. Here, we can see many aspects of that film turning into shorthand clichés that ironically can be used to advertise technology-dependent global multi-nationalism: a fascination with elemental forms and forces (the light of the setting sun, the poetic glow of the bonfire); an expression of mystery and even of the mystical that implies deeper secrets to the universe (as Paquin lists the miracles of new communication, her voice fills with wonder, her eyes open wide in amazement, her face offers the most meagre hint of an enigmatic smile); an intimation that we can enter a mythic realm (the 'virtual journey to any moment in time') in which 'normal' physical laws of being are to be suspended (the mythic journey here being provided by new technology); a sense of life's deeper meanings as radiating through forms of affect (the music, the dance), rather than through rationality alone. There's even an echo of *The Piano*'s enlistment (and for some critics, exploitation) of images of indigenous people as indexes of the exotic and ineffable mystery. The quick shot of the 'native' man hints at a timelessness while establishing indigenous culture as so obviously 'primitive' that it cannot enter the technologically modernised world (the 'native' does not speak, is not shown to have access to the promises of a media revolution that is indicated as having the potential to unify sites of advanced capitalism – for example, New York, Tokyo, France). *The Piano* here becomes an inspiring source for an intensely mythic and yet modern appropriation.

And the fact that *The Piano* stands for something special and does so in stylistically and thematically special ways – namely, the representation of womanly sensibility – can also make it a target for a re-masculinising disdain that would like to take a distance from all things feminine. For instance, in Kevin Smith's sophomoric comedy version of religious (or anti-religious) allegory, *Dogma* (1999), a battle between a lapsed angel (Ben Affleck) and two totally cool grunge dudes on a sacred mission is punctuated and resolved by the cataclysmic appearance of God on the scene. God is represented as a mysterious woman (played by rock star Alanis Morissette) with a Mona Lisa smile and bountiful pre-Raphaelite tresses of curly hair and dressed in a long flowing gown. This feminine God does not speak but moves through the battleground and makes miracles happen through ineffable mystery. The Gen-X dudes express relief at God's salvation of the world, but also guy-culture's impatience with her silence and enigmatic countenance (manifested by the knowing but unrevealing smile on her face that suggests her prepossessed grasp of the deep nature of things). As one of the two dudes angrily wonders, 'What the fuck is this? *The Piano*? Why isn't this broad talking?'

For better or worse, *The Piano* has become the symbol of what the 1990s came to term 'the chick flick'. As such, it could be used to symbolise a range of emotions and experiences associated with a feminine realm. Thus, in a moment of comic irony on the television show, *Dharma and Greg* – about a couple from varied backgrounds (his family is wealthy and waspy, her parents are hippies) – Greg realises that he doesn't know much about the personal emotional life of his gruff, reserved father and gets Dharma to charm the father into answering biographical questions. When they pore over the results, Greg is surprised to discover that his father has listed *The Piano* as his favourite film, since this choice does not seem in keeping with his father's conservative, no-nonsense masculinised approach to life. But Dharma then explains that the father picked this film since, for him, it reduces down to the story of a mute woman stuck on an island, an obvious wish-fulfilment image for how he'd like women, including his own wife, to be: silent and confined.[2]

The success of Campion's film makes it a key work in our historical moment. Both in the ways it was marketed in the global independent film business and in the ways this marketing was matched by the resonances its story and style seem to have had for many viewers, *The Piano* marks something special in the history of non-Hollywood cinema (even as it perhaps makes overtures to Hollywood, as we'll see). The overall statistics are telling. Jane Campion's two feature films before *The Piano*, *Sweetie* and *An Angel at My Table*, each made around $1 million in the US market, and £136,962 and £365,805 respectively in the British market. (According to the Australian Film Commission, *The Piano* made AUD 11.2 million in its release there, while *Sweetie* made 4 million.) *Sweetie* and *An Angel at My Table* were independent foreign films, distributed in very limited ways with limited promotional campaigns to a niche market of art-film audiences – the resultant box office for them is not surprising. In parallel fashion, Campion's two feature films after *The Piano*, *The Portrait of a Lady* and *Holy Smoke*, were not mass-market box-office successes, the former making a little less than $4 million in the USA and the latter a little less than $2 million (in Australia *Holy Smoke* made AUD1.4 million). The UK revenue was £681,082 for *The Portrait of a Lady* and £323,851 for *Holy Smoke*. (To put the implication of such box-office results in perspective, it might be noted that *The Portrait of a Lady*'s budget was US$30 million.)

But *The Piano*, while costing between $7 and $8 million to produce, made over US$40 million in the US market (it was the tenth highest grossing film of 1993), AUD12,328,604 in Australia, £4,848,517 in the UK, and more than US$100 million worldwide. For a foreign film released by an independent distributor, this certainly easily qualifies as a smash hit. *The Piano* stands out in Campion's career as a major commercial sensation, one that moved beyond art-film audiences to cross over into a mainstream market.[3]

This financial success was matched by a success on the awards circuit. The recognition started with the film's appearance at the Cannes Film Festival where it won a Best Actress award for Holly Hunter and shared the Palme d'Or (the highest award) with the Chinese film, *Farewell My Concubine*. This represents the first time in the Cannes festival's history that a woman director won the top award. On its release in the New Zealand-born Campion's adopted country Australia, the film swept the Australian Film Institute awards, winning in eleven categories out of thirteen. In several countries, it revealingly won the Best Foreign Picture award (for example, this is the one category that it placed in at the César awards, France's parallel to the Oscars), but in the USA, undoubtedly because of its crossover success and its use of English language and American stars, it was clearly treated by the big award organisations less as a foreign film than as a mainstream film with a proper and appropriate place in the context of US film distribution and exhibition. Thus, it was nominated for a very impressive eight Oscars (Best Picture – a category that has admitted only a few foreign films during the history of the Oscars – Best Director, Best Original Screenplay, Best Editing, Best Cinematography, Best Costume Design, Best Actress, Best Supporting Actress) with Holly Hunter and Anna Paquin winning the Best Actress and Best Supporting Actress awards respectively, and Campion herself winning the Best Original Screenplay award. (The Best Film, Best Direction, Best Editing and Best Cinematography awards that year all went to *Schindler's List*.) We might also note that *The Piano* received great intellectual or scholarly attention (as witnessed in the bibliography to this

Cartoon. Reproduced by courtesy of Paul Zanetti, Paul Zanetti Illustrations

volume). Campion's earlier films got some reviews and had a few essays devoted to them (some in Australian publications that evidently wanted to applaud what they saw as a new voice in Australian film-making). The later films get a fair number of reviews – as if critics felt impelled to judge if Campion could keep up her success after *The Piano* – and understandably, there is a dossier on *The Portrait of a Lady* in *The Henry James Review*. But to a much greater extent than the other films, *The Piano* receives discussion in the form of anthologies and critical essays. It is certainly a film that many people have felt impelled to write about (often for very affective and personal reasons, as we'll see).

Since its release in 1993, *The Piano* has come to be seen as one of the supreme signposts of the art of feminine sensibility. (For the moment, I would like to bracket out the question of the relationship of such sensibility to a more specifically *feminist* one.) While, as we will see, a focus on the feminine from a particular perspective of affect and personal suffering can also be said to characterise the earlier films of Jane Campion, the rich emotionalism of *The Piano* seemed, to many cinema-goers, to herald something new in the director's career and even in the overall cultural history of woman's representation. This film divides the career of its director. As a consequence, a traditional authorial analysis which would look at thematic continuities and artistic refinements in the unfolding of an overall aesthetic project crashes up against discontinuity, against the fragmentation of an *oeuvre*. This disjunction fuels much of the concern in the following pages to offer a close stylistic analysis of the films that Campion has signed. The purpose is not to find in each film a richness that can then be treated as a progressive unfolding of an overall genius; rather, it is to pinpoint the material particularity of each of the films and resist their assimilation to an expressive aesthetic that would need to see them as interconnected emanations of an artistic spirit. While we might not want to go to the extent of fully disavowing the director as deliberative agent in the work of film production – as did much of the anti-auteurist film theory of the 1970s – we need to put directorial agency in its proper place, seeing it as one factor only in stylistic and thematic decision.

Two
Desiring the Director

> The process of the writing [of a life] may be set down as simply as laying down a main trunk line from Then to Now, with branch excursions into the outlying wilderness, but the real shape, the first shape, is always a circle formed only to be broken and reformed again.
>
> Janet Frame, *An Angel at My Table*

The place of the director is a divided one – divided, for instance, internally by the complexities of the psyche (against authorship as conscious intention, psychoanalysis reminds us of all that is unconscious and even conflictual in expressions of will, intention, desire, deliberative agency), but also divided by social forces that mean that the director's voice is only one among many (the many others who work on the film, but also the many who distribute and promote the film and the many who consume it, all according to their own social agencies and agendas).

Indeed, in a general survey of issues in director studies today, film scholars Toby Miller and Noel King take the case of Jane Campion as showing some of the problems of assuming that the director's voice and vision offer an exclusive explanation of the significance of films:

> [W]e can ask how the Australian-based New Zealand film-maker Jane Campion was pronounced an auteur. After having directed a feature film, a mini-series, and a handful of shorts, Campion was said, with *Sweetie* (1989), to possess a distinct connotative stamp, a set of concerns about the power in the everyday and the underside of life, the abject, that which is best evaded and ignored. The smallest units of audiovisual style were taken as signs and symptoms of this vision: framing, tilts, cutaways, visual jokes, and music. ... But what happens to these auteurist certainties when we turn to the figure of Gerard Lee, who wrote and co-directed the 'Campion' short, *Passionless Moments* (1983/84) and who co-wrote the screenplay of *Sweetie*, based on personal experience? Or when we turn to Sally Bongers, the director of

> photography who has a distinctive style of lighting and framing that puts energy into set-ups rather than camera movements? It's an enduring problem for auteurism to distinguish between these industrial and personal identities and their responsibility for texts.[1]

We need to take such cautions to heart. To study a career means today to avoid imagining a creativity that derives from individual genius or talent. To argue that films by a certain director have some stylistic regularities or even some regularities of subject matter would have to take place without assigning unified meaningful connotations to them, including even the connotations of personal vision.

It is, I would imagine, always possible with a group of objects (such as a series of films) to come up with some qualities they share (especially as one moves higher and higher into generalities). In the case of films signed by one director, it is tempting to imagine that because they share this signature, they must consequently and inevitably share other qualities (for example, stylistic regularities, thematic meanings) – what Miller and King refer to as 'connotative stamp' – and that pinpointing and appreciating these should be the goal of critical activity. But it is this temptation that can be resisted: the director can, for instance, be studied not as a source of aesthetic distinction but as an effect, a series of meanings attributed to the director by cinema-goers and by other users (for example, film distributors). Thus, in some of the pages of this study, I will be concerned less with what Campion films 'mean' than with what various 'user-groups', such as the emotive fans of *The Piano*, take them to 'mean'. It would seem critically benign to imagine that various works by an artist might exhibit continuities. The questions this raises, though, are what critical status we give to these continuities and what causal explanation we offer for them. (To take one of my favourite examples, B-director Arthur Lubin went from directing 'Francis the Talking Mule' films in the late 1940s to turning out episodes of the talking horse series *Mr Ed* in the 1950s, but one would probably want to see such regularities not as 'symptoms' of a personal vision but rather as demonstrations of the pressures and constraints of the production system for hack directors. At best, one wouldn't want to *interpret* the regularities in

Lubin's career so much as account for the impersonal institutional and industrial reasons for their existence. And in that case, the fact of regularity would not easily be the basis of an affirmative aesthetic judgment; that is, the career is not more artistically valuable because it is regularised. To refer to an 'Arthur Lubin film' is not to speak of a source of meaning or aesthetic value: 'Arthur Lubin' in this case is not the name of an author but refers instead to the operations of a production system and the non-creative role B-directors were assigned within it. 'Arthur Lubin' is the name for a lack of authorship.)

It is possible, then, to imagine that regularities in a career could be disconnected from any concern with an individualised personal vision. With respect to Miller and King, for instance, we might imagine that the recurrent look of Campion films derives as much from other people who worked on them (people she often chose to work with). And we would then want to be open to the possibility that the various workers on a film could internalise each other's stylistic or thematic preoccupations to such a degree that nothing in the film could really univocally be assigned to this or that person individually. For example, even when Sally Bongers doesn't work on a Campion film, it might be the case that it has some of the 'Bongers' look. Influence does not always derive just from immediate contribution. (In the Conclusion, I return to some specific concrete cases in which Campion's work as an author blurs or blends with other authors.)

The name of 'Jane Campion' has mattered in particular to many people because it is a woman's name and can refer thereby to the complicated destiny of the female artist, especially in a domain such as the cinema so frequently dominated by men. In the 1950s, when film criticism sought to treat directors as the auteurs (authors) of their films, the emphasis tended to be on male directors – treated as veritable heroes – who by force of will, commitment to a vision, sagacity and energetic force managed, against the pressures of the studio system, to imprint their identity on films. For example, US critic Manny Farber's classic essay from 1957, 'Underground Movies', on action directors such as William Wellman and Howard Hawks, has as its not-so-hidden subtext a desire to shore up a particularly virile image of tough masculinity and to promote directors of brute determination, rather than those of liberal sensibility or sensitivity (Farber's example of the latter is Fred Zinnemann with *High Noon* or *The Nun's Story*).

In recent years, to a large degree under the influence of feminism, there has been an attempt in film study to examine the hitherto neglected careers of women directors. For example, there have been full-length books devoted to Alice Guy, Dorothy Arzner and Ida Lupino. Inevitably, the study of the woman director has to eschew some of the mythology of virile heroism that distinguished the earlier attention to male directors: for instance, in her book on Dorothy Arzner, Judith Mayne emphasises how that director was far from the image of the rugged loner individualist that distinguished male auteurism, living and working as she did with a necessary dependence on a community of other women. In her very work ethic, Arzner, as Mayne depicts her, deeply felt the need for bonding and emotional connection, and this, Mayne argues, inspires the Arzner films themselves, which are often about communities of women.[2]

Despite Campion's own often ambiguous relationship to feminism –

Campion on the set of *Sweetie*

reflected, for instance, in the debates around the sexual and racial politics of *The Piano* – and despite the temptations that director study runs of falling into myths of personal vision, it can be of polemical usefulness to study her career. Campion's career shows, in the very tensions it exhibits, some of the options open to women artists and the expectations placed upon them within a complex cultural sphere such as that of global art cinema.

Rather than as the signature or symptom of a unified vision, it might be best then to treat the name 'Jane Campion' as signalling what French philosopher Michel Foucault terms a space of 'dispersion' – the name of the author as a shorthand for all the forces that work against unity, against the career as a coherent unfolding of a vision.[3] There is, for instance, as the example of cinematographer Sally Bongers suggests, the dispersion of authorial responsibility among the many members of the production team so that paradoxically to call a work a 'Jane Campion' film may be to recognise how she helps facilitate work communities where various contributors can all make their mark. But there is also a dispersion to the career itself: even as most of the films signed by Campion centre on women's experience – often a cruelly depicted one in which women bear the brunt of the world's potential for violence – there are variations, even contradictions, in tone and treatment of this experience from film to film.

Again, it is for this reason that the following pages involve close readings of the films: the point is less to catalogue recurrences of style than to chart divergences. First, there are divergences between style and subject matter that complicate simple associations of Campion's films with a singular vision (for example, a vision centred on a feminist intepretation of everyday existence). For instance, several of the early films deal with real-life issues – especially issues of personal safety and sanctity – that confront women, but the weird style of these films can have the effect of making these issues one more example of a curious surreality (what we might call the David Lynchian aspect of Campion's early films) that finally seems more absurd than realist. In the very estranging effects of their style, the films can work to turn real-life dilemmas into modernist symbols of ambiguity (was there, for instance, incest between Gordon and his daughter in the film *Sweetie*?; was the heroine of the early short *A Girl's Own Story* actually molested?). Just as the study of women directors can serve as a corrective to the masculinising and heroicising trend of auteurism, so too does a reminder of subject matter that deals with women's issues help to eschew formalist positions that would see film as little more than experimental play with no real-life purchase and thereby help us understand how spectators can find great emotional resonances in the Campion films.

In the case, for instance, of *The Piano*, close analysis of its treatment of subject matter is useful because fans have clearly identified the film as being about issues of selfhood and sexual identity; at the same time, stylistic analysis can pinpoint the ways in which the film formally constructs its appeal and, for some critics as we'll see, does so at the cost of obscuring issues around race and sexual violence.

Films are commodities that circulate through markets from producers to consumers. As such, they can be treated within a political economy that takes the specific traits of any individual item for sale as less important than market pressures, advertising efforts, organisation and defence of means of distribution and codified rules of consumption (for example, in the Golden Age of Hollywood cinema, many people went to the movies not for individual titles but out of a generalised desire for Hollywood entertainment). At the same time, it is clear that different classes of films circulate differently: markets are about the production of value, and there are diverse strategies for attributing value to this or that individual film. For instance, writing of the international art cinema that gained such attention from urban professionals in the 1950s and 1960s, film scholar Thomas Elsaesser suggests that international film festivals were one of the key institutions for differentiating films (those that were selected versus those that were not; those that won prizes versus those that came away empty-handed) and assigning value to them. As Elsaesser puts it, 'festivals are the markets that can fix and assign different kinds of value, from touristic, politico-voyeuristic curiosity to auteur-status, and set in motion the circulation of new cultural capital, beyond the prospect of economic circulation (art cinema distribution, a television sale)'.[4] Certainly, the festival venue has been important to the circulation of Campion's films through culture.

While close analysis of individual film works could never fully account for the ways in which institutions and communities (including the community of spectators) involved in the circulation of film commodities determine which films will be accorded differential value, it can be useful as a way of suggesting some of the traits that are commonly picked up and promoted in this or that form of distribution and consumption. For instance, while user-communities, such as fans, had a great deal to do with the success of *The Piano*, there were certain traits in this film that allowed it to be attended to in this way, that encouraged an affective bonding onto it. Close analysis can have a place within political economy for its precise attention to the elements that make up the film-commodity, and that may be actualised or attended to by an institution participating in its circulation. Where some film scholars have seen close analysis as an alternative to interpretation of film in relation to cultural context,[5] and where political economists have sometimes implied that markets are so effective they overpower the attraction (or not) of specific commodities, close analysis can be a useful stage in the study of texts in the ways they circulate through society, and in some cases do so in special ways (as, for instance, in the case of the art film). As French cultural critic Roland Barthes said in a famous declaration, 'a little formalism turns one away from History, but a lot brings one back to it'.[6]

It is necessary then to also examine divergences between style and subject together *and* their reception by cinema-goers. To take one example, it does seem that *The Portrait of a Lady* was a film carefully planned – by its director, its scriptwriter, its cinematographer, and so on – to match a story of entrapment with a visual style of confinement. *The Portrait of a Lady* is a heavily designed film, and moments that diverge from this overriding claustrophobic design – for example, scenes of heavy eroticism, moments of fantasy, attempts to suggest liberation through tilted shots – were generally received by critics as inconsistencies that stood out from the film. At the same time, ironically, it was the very fact that the film so matched its overriding style and subject that also led to it disappointing those viewers who wanted a different – more romantic – story and a less claustrophobic style. Content analysis and formal analysis thereby link up with a study of audience expectations and desires.

In the late 1960s and 1970s, cultural theory began to talk of 'the death of the author', taking that phrase from the title of a very influential essay by Roland Barthes. But in his 1969 essay, 'What is an Author?' (often cited along with Barthes's as ammunition for a critique of the appeal of author study), Michel Foucault argued that even if one wants to analyse aspects of culture other than the author, it is still necessary to understand why a fascination with assigning works back to the authors has been so persistent in our approaches to artistic works. For Foucault, the author is not so much a fixed entity through which we always explain an artistic work (as he notes, there are historical moments that celebrate anonymous works or works with fictive authors, such as Homer) but what he calls an author-function. That is, a concern with authorship comes into play when a society finds it useful, functional, to treat artistic works as authored. Societies could function without notions of the author, but there is still the fact that in so much of contemporary culture, there has been historically a desire to imagine authors, to give unity to creative careers and assign meaning to that. In Foucault's words,

> [T]he presence of an author's name is functional in that it serves as a means of classification. A name can group together a number of texts and thus differentiate them from others. A name also establishes different forms of relationships among texts. ... [T]he author's name characterises a particular manner of existence of discourse. Discourse that possesses an author's name is not to be immediately consumed and forgotten; neither is it accorded the momentary attention given to ordinary, fleeting words. Rather, its status and its manner of reception are regulated by the culture in which it circulates. ... In this sense, the function of an author is to characterise the existence, circulation, and operation of certain discourses within a society.[7]

What functions are served, then, by taking a number of films (and perhaps novels) to which Jane Campion contributed and attributing them to her *as author*? As Foucault suggests, by assigning an author to certain works, we differentiate them from others: in this respect, we might note how in the complicated field of film distribution, the singling out of 'Campion' can give her a certain cultural capital as a director of artistically distinctive or ambitious films, of films that offer something other than standard Hollywood fare (with one recurrent criticism of *The Portrait of a Lady* being that it does not diverge far enough: for example, John Malkovich's performance was seen by some critics not to differ from other maniacal figures he has played in Hollywood productions). The study of the director mutates then into a study of the reception of the idea of the director and the ways that elements in the films can contribute to this idea. Thus, in a sharp critique of *The Piano*, feminist scholar Carol Clover argues that the film obscures its investment in woman's enslavement in an oppressive mechanics of exchange (sex for piano keys) by veiling its subject matter in the aestheticising trappings of the high-art film. For Clover, a look at the audience – and how it constructs a film's value – has the salutary effect of removing the film from its ivory-tower privilege and turning it into an object for practical use among its target community. As Clover notes,

> One of the odder features of American film criticism is its habit of looking at genre films in terms of audience response (a response it frequently decries) but art films in terms of authorial intention. Whereas we acknowledge genre films as collective fantasies (and judge them accordingly), art films we see as something like illustrated philosophy.[8]

To examine the function of an art film director for his or her audience, then, is to move away from a conception of the director as an origin of meanings and attitudes to one in which meanings and attitudes are imputed to the director in the reception of him or her. The art film is a cultural activity which circulates among concrete users in a fully social world. In Clover's analysis, it is as if the film of artistic ambition is brought back to earth, rendered accessible to a material study of its circulation in culture.

Here we would also need to examine how the differentiating value attributed to Campion films can vary over the course of the career: in the USA at least, the early films were distributed to the quite specific niche of the art-film crowd, while *The Piano* and *Portrait of a Lady* were presented as works of uplifting prestige, important films that a general cultured public should see rather than as modest little experimental works. Thus, in the 1990s, the US independent producer and distributor Miramax began to push aggressively for certain of its films – both the ones it had financed and the ones it had picked up from other production sources – to gain the attention both of an art-film critical establishment and of a general public concerned with entertainment: the award-winning *Pulp Fiction*, *The Piano* and *Shakespeare in Love* are obvious beneficiaries of Miramax's attempts to promote films to 'crossover' from art cinemas to the mainstream of film exhibition. *The Piano* appears to have mattered to Miramax because the film fitted new commercial requirements placed on independent feature films in the 1990s. In an article on the new economics of the 1990s art film, cinema historian Tino Balio recounts Miramax's handling of the film in this fashion:

> A cultural hodge-podge financed by the French company CiBy 2000, filmed in New Zealand by a native-born writer-director with an international cast, and having Australian nationality by dint of its Sydney-based producer, Jan Chapman, *The Piano* was acquired [by Miramax] weeks before it was shown at Cannes where it won the Palme d'Or. *Newsweek* devoted a two-page article and a full-page photo to *The Piano*, describing the 'delirious standing ovation' after its screening and the 'fever pitch' of the reception a full six months before the picture was released in the US.[9]

Combining the uplifting traits of the prestige film (and in particular of the sub-genre of the costume drama) with the enigmatic traits of European art cinema (ambiguous symbolism, unexplained character background, and so on) but balancing these with a mass-market accessibility (through named stars and a forward-moving narrative that ultimately was not all that ambiguous) and sensationalism (explicit sexuality, extreme violence), *The Piano* participates in a refashioning of the art film for the 1990s. For example, Thomas Elsaesser argues that a number of directors – and he specifically cites Campion as one of these – contribute to a shift in the art film from the probing positing of questions to a showing off of cinematic talent and striking visual form. As he puts it, the new concern of the art film is 'not self-doubt nor self-expression, not metaphysical themes or a realist aesthetic' but 'command of the generic, the expressive, the excessive, the visual, and the visceral ... valued for their capacity to concentrate on a tour de force'.[10]

Miramax, specifically, becomes a key player in a redefinition of the independent art film to one that maintains superficial traits of art cinema while making it more palatable for wider global distribution and frequently allows crossover into a mass market. It is important to note that the company is a subsidiary of one of the biggest global players in entertainment, Disney, and enables the parent company to reach new niche audiences (for example, those spectators who want something more adult from their cinema) and thereby find new means to gain value for their commodities. (I have heard it claimed by players in the independent film business that each film Miramax decides to get behind makes it harder for ten less-supported and promoted independent films to gain distribution and exhibition.) Miramax, in particular, is key in constructing the possibilities for a new sub-genre of the art film, summed up by three of its successes, *The Piano*, *Shakespeare in Love* and *Chocolat*. Whatever their individual differences, these films are all primarily chronological narratives focused on a central character who battles for self-expression in an environment of oppression or, rather, repression (that is, the restrictions on the individual are primarily directed against self-expression, personal artistry or talent, and self-realisation). Against repression, the films hold out the possibility of a salvation through commitment to one's desires and through love (and in each case, the man who comes into a woman's life is a relative outsider to dominant power) and they play on patterns of inspiration and romantic transcendence (these are films that, no matter how bad things get for the protagonist, are still insistent on a feel-good uplift). They use international casts both to appeal to a number of national audiences and to advertise their own artistic ambition (for example, the use of Geoffrey Rush, winner of an Oscar for the art film *Shine*, in *Shakespeare in Love*).

The undecidability of Campion's provenance – is she a New Zealander?; an Australian?; do her films belong to one national cinema or the other? – may actually be in keeping with the new needs of art-cinema promotion. There has indeed been debate about Campion's relation to national cinema. For instance, while many writers treat Campion as Australian with *The Piano* serving as a key work by which that national cinema can reach out to international art-cinema markets, New Zealand critic Peter Calder emphatically inscribes the film within New Zealand nationhood:

> Most of its supporting cast and virtually all the crew were locals. Its theme – the collision of female sensibility with pioneer pragmatism – may not be uniquely antipodean but it has been and remains a preoccupation of our art, especially our literature. From its opening frames, shot on the surf-lashed Auckland west coast beach of Karekare, its mise-en-scène placed it in an aesthetic realm which we instantly recognized – and which the world would come to know – as unmistakably New Zealand.[11]

Just as strongly, the film has been proclaimed an Australian work. One solution, which Tom O'Regan in *Australian National Cinema* offers, is to suggest how markets force a move from national cinemas to larger contexts:

> Campion's explicitly Australian based work is sometimes claimed for New Zealand cinema. *Sweetie* was screened in Sydney as part of a festival of New Zealand cinema. Is Campion a New Zealander or an Australian? ... Does her work spanning the Tasmanian sea . . . presage the development of a more integrated 'Australasian' film market to undergird an Australasian identity? *The Piano* was set in New Zealand and made by a New Zealand director and of its three principals two were American and one a New Zealander. The Australian connection is solely that the AFC provided Campion with script development money and that Campion is Sydney-based, has lived in Australia for seventeen years, was trained at the AFTRS [Australian Film, Television and Radio School], and has used Australian film subsidy and production regimes to develop her talent and film properties. Yet *The Piano* is not simply another international production with some Australian involvement, it also represents Australasian film-making and a growing convergence and integration of the Australian and New Zealand film-making, exhibition and distribution sectors in the 1990s.[12]

In an oft-cited article on the origins of art cinema, scholar Steven Neale treats it in terms of various national cinemas struggling for self-definition.[13] But it may as much be the case in the recent global market that art cinema – along with some of the national popular cinemas – is presented as not tied to indigenous styles and subject matters or, even more, involves turning indigenous forms into signs of local colour that is internationally saleable. Where, for instance, some commentators have treated *Sweetie* in terms of a specifically Australian inflection in the representation of suburban life as a sort of grotesquerie, the Miramax-distributed *Holy Smoke* turns Australia (as it does India) into a form of exoticism, a place where people from various cultures can come together and discover possibilities of self-reinvention. Trashy suburbia still comes in for ridicule, but Australian suburban life is now treated as something local and transitional, something out-of-touch (the vulgar wife who just doesn't get what's going on around her), something to be left behind as one moves on in the world (literally). If *Sweetie* ends with the surviving characters resuming their Australian ways of life, *Holy Smoke*, in contrast, concludes with its central characters off in other parts of the globe (P. J. is back in the USA, Ruth is in India where even her mother, so previously caught up in provincial resistance to other cultures, has joined her). For all its return to an Australian setting, *Holy Smoke* is a post-national film, forming a divide between the place where one is born and the movements to new sites in which one lives out one's life.

Campion herself is in some ways already a post-national figure, ready to take up a role in the global film scene. Significantly, *The Piano* and the two films that follow it (*The Portrait of a Lady* and *Holy Smoke*) all deal with figures from one culture coming to another, with resultant cultural clashes, stories of uprooting and an inability to find one's place. We might contrast these later works with *An Angel at My Table* where Janet Frame does travel abroad but triumphantly returns home, literally putting on the shoes of the father and assuming an identity as a national and nationally rooted writer. In the later films, in fact, home is something one only temporarily inhabits – both the homes one grew up in and the homes one moves to. Movement, transport, migration and interactions between cultures have become recurrent visual tropes in numerous works of recent global cinema, and the internationally financed Campion films participate in the elaboration of an emergent form of cinema, developing new subject matter and new stylistic tropes (for example, the recurrence of images of voyage through and across cultures, as in the constant in-motion activity of characters in the films of

Hong Kong director Wong Kar-Wai). Even the curious casting details of some recent art films – Harvey Keitel as a Scotsman in *The Piano*, John Gielgud as Mr Touchett in *The Portrait of a Lady* (in the novel, he's decidedly American), Juliette Binoche in *Chocolat* as a French woman who speaks English exclusively – are part of a global marketing in which individual national belongings are blurred together. This is a phenomenon with a long history in the art cinema – think, for instance, of the international co-productions of the 1950s or 1960s that led, for instance, to Burt Lancaster playing an Italian patriarch in several films. But the recent art film adds a new inflection by emphasising a mutability of identity, an ease by which characters can move through roles and geographic spaces.

The following pages set out then to describe some of the diversity in Jane Campion's career while suggesting how the pressures of the market increasingly push that career in pointed directions. I take *The Piano* as dividing the career and so begin with it. I then 'flashback' to the early films and deal subsequently with the last films and announced upcoming projects. As noted before, the Conclusion picks up some issues of authorship by looking at Campion's work as a writer.

Three
Dividing Lines

If, as we've seen, *The Piano*'s veritable incarnation of a sensibility can make it stand as an easy stereotype of certain cultural norms of feelings and emotions, and open it to parody or appropriation, it is clear also that the film can marshal extreme and extremely positive outpourings of affect. Many women, in particular, attest to a profound, intense bonding with *The Piano*, a strong sense of connection in which the effusive affect of the relationship of spectator to screen is insisted upon. Take, for instance, just some of the testimonials to *The Piano* that show up on an Internet chat group devoted to it:

> I saw it, i was under my feelings and fell into a sea of emotions that i hadn't discovered. It's heart breaking and takes away my reality. ... its sadness and emotion make it an unforgettable movie which it's going to be in the eternity until good and real feelings are over.
>
> It touched me deeply and I'm obsessed with it, I've seen it so many times I particularly love the tone of Ada's voice in the beginning, her inner strength and the warmth of the scenes in the house because of the light orange color.
>
> *The Piano* is the best movie I have ever seen. It moved me like no other movie could. ... The symbolism is so deep and the movie has a profound spirituality to it. *The Piano* is more than a movie, it's an experience.
>
> *The Piano* is my favourite film. I have seen it 94 times (I keep a tally) ... This film is absolutely note-perfect.[1]

And lest we assume that such outpourings of affect come exclusively from a general audience responding to the cinematic experience with sentiment rather than critical perspective, we might note the extent to which a strong part of the scholarly or professional critical commentary on the film not merely speaks of the film's resonant emotionalism but literally speaks it – that is, invests in an affective power of *The Piano* and uses critical discourse as a way to continue the writer's bond(ing) with the film. Criticism in such cases glides into personal testimony and even a merging of spectator with film.

A revealing example of the way in which the film leads some scholarly critics to intensely personal testimony of emotional connection is an essay by film scholar Vivian Sobchack, 'What My Fingers Knew: The Cinesthetic Subject, or Vision in the Flesh'.[2] This is a work of general film theory in which Sobchack challenges the ways in which traditionally such theory has opted for analytic abstractions that encourage distance from filmic works rather than affective connection to them, what she describes as 'the gap that exists between our actual *experience* of the cinema and the *theory* that we academic film scholars write to explain it – or perhaps, more aptly, to explain it away'. In her effort to give concreteness to a theory of what happens affectively and physically when we go to the movies, *The Piano* is a central piece of evidence through which Sobchack can testify to her own emotional investments:

> I want to ground my previous discussion 'in the flesh.' In *my* flesh, in fact – and its meaningful responsiveness to and comprehension of an actual film, here *The Piano*. However intellectually problematic in terms of its sexual and colonial politics, Campion's film moved me deeply, stirring my bodily senses and my sense of my body. The film not only 'filled me up' and often 'suffocated' me with feelings that resonated in and constricted my chest and stomach, but it also 'sensitized' the very surfaces of my skin – as well as its own – to *touch*. Throughout the film, my whole being was intensely concentrated and, rapt as I was in the world on-screen, I was wrapped also in a body that was achingly aware of itself as a sensuous, sensitized, sensible material capacity. ... I would argue that my experience of *The Piano* was a heightened instance of our common sensuous experience of the movies: the way we are in some carnal modality able to touch and be touched by the substance and texture of images; to feel a visual atmosphere envelop us; to experience weight, suffocation, and the need for air; to take flight in kinetic exhilaration and freedom even as we are relatively bound to our theater seats; to be knocked backwards by a sound; to sometimes even smell and taste the world we see upon the screen.

What about *The Piano* makes it lend itself so extensively to intense emotional investment? I would suggest that we can pinpoint some of the qualities that *The Piano* embodies – and perhaps exemplifies – and that may account for much of its highly affective appeal by seeing it as one embodiment of what has come to be known as the 'woman's film'. In particular, I will contend, as a film in large part about a woman who gains new forms of self-expression by taking control of the erotic dimension of her life, *The Piano* enacts a narrative of romantic longing and redemption that we can associate with one form of the woman's film: the Gothic romance – narratives of a menaced woman saved by the love of a man. Among other things, such a discussion might provide us with one way to approach the range of Campion's films: if *The Piano* has been taken by many spectators as a signpost of a new possibility of the representation of affect and sensibility on-screen, it is also possible that the film may stand in comparable fashion as a sign of a unique moment in Campion's career. Later, I'll discuss how the notion of the 'woman's film' has come to stand for a variety of approaches to cultural representation so that no one work can be seen as incarnating the form. In particular, there has been a call – most famously represented in Laura Mulvey's 1975 essay 'Visual Pleasure and Narrative Cinema' – for a new combative form of the woman's film that would refuse an erotic treatment of women and break down traditional forms of cinematic pleasure. The force and function of the other films signed by Campion may lie in their development of other models of feminine being than the fundamentally romantic and erotic, and we need to outline the specific traits of their particular appeal. (At the same time, we will see how *The Piano* has become an open text that defenders, in particular, can always interpret in new ways, so that there has evolved a 'Mulveyan' defence of the film as a deconstruction of the erotic representation of Woman.)

While Campion garnered critical attention even early on – as in Freda Freiberg's essay on 'The Bizarre in the Banal: Notes on the Films of Jane Campion', published *before* the release of *Sweetie*, her first feature film (other than the made-for-TV *Two Friends*)[3] – and while some critics note a continuity of concerns, even around affect and emotional intensity, across the range of her films, it is apparent that for many spectators *The Piano* represents the emergence of something new and unique in the history of romantic cinema. In this respect, as I posited before, the film divides Campion's career. Just as we can examine the connection (and dis-connection) of her earlier films to *The Piano*, so too we need to be aware of the ways in which the film's success has effects on Campion's work since then. For instance, there was great expectation around *The Portrait of a Lady*, her next film, and the fact that many people perceived it as not re-creating the feel of *The Piano* no doubt accounts for much of the negative reaction to this later film.

What is the woman's film of romantic longing and redemption, and how might *The Piano* offer some of the pleasures of that genre? Recently, in an important book in film studies, *Film/Genre*, film theorist Rick Altman has challenged the notion that the identity of genre films lies in the films themselves, in objective qualities that one can catalogue.[4] In contrast, Altman argues for what he calls a 'pragmatic' approach to genre, an approach that posits how genres are created out of needs – for example, the needs of a critical establishment, of a movie-going public, of institutions of film production (for example, the publicity branches of the studios) to organise and classify films among themselves in one way as opposed to another. Significantly, Altman uses the 'woman's film' as one primary example in order to study how a genre is constructed out of the function it fulfils. As he shows, the woman's film came to be talked about when the needs of a cultural moment – for instance, the feminist concern to study positive and negative implications of feminine representation – encouraged it to be talked about.

But it is necessary, I would contend, to imagine that in most cases genre classification, though a pragmatic act, is based on an identification of objective traits in individual works even though these traits in no way necessitate genre classification (that is, just because a group of works share some traits doesn't mean we automatically make a genre out of them). In other words, genre classifications are based on elements actually *in* the works, although it is only the pragmatic decision to notice, privilege and compare them from film to film that creates a genre. The common traits become significant only when the classifier chooses to emphasise them. For instance, a number of films may be set in the old West, but they come to constitute the genre of the Western only when someone chooses to make that connection between the films (and convinces others to share in the discovery of the genre). Another genre classification might choose to pinpoint other traits in the same works (thus, some elements of a film might lead to one's calling it a Western, while others might lead to one's calling it, say, a 'Clint Eastwood' film). At the same time, however, it would be hard (although, I imagine, not impossible) to constitute a genre if none of the individual works were found to have the pertinent trait (thus, for instance, it would be hard to deem a work a 'Clint Eastwood' film if Eastwood had had nothing to do with it). The woman's film derives from the pragmatic effects of scholar-viewers, but these viewers construct the genre out of elements in the films that they deem relevant and, particularly in the case of this genre, forge intensely affective connections to. Here, again, we find a place for close analysis as it enables us to be precise about those traits that were activated by its users. *The Piano*, for instance, had features that met pragmatic needs for romantic cinema, and to offer a close analysis of those features is thereby a way already to enter into issues of reception. Moreover, to say this is not to assume those needs necessarily derive from any sort of deep-seated desire within the hearts of spectators; it is, for instance, clear also that needs can be manufactured, solicited, incited – for example, by promotional campaigns. *The Piano* circulates through the film market, and at each step, there are user-communities who adjudicate the meaning and impact of the work.

I want to introduce the pertinent traits that situate *The Piano* in relation to other romantic works of feminine longing by looking at three scenes from the film. These three sequences all involve people looking at or longing for the piano. The first occurs early in the film when Stewart (Sam Neill) tells the newly arrived Ada she must leave her piano on the beach because there are not enough men to carry it through the jungle. A shot through the legs of the piano shows Stewart trying, somewhat ineffectually, to round up the Maori men cavorting on the beach and start them on the journey back to his property. The lush well-known theme song of the film begins in this shot only to well up all the more in the next, a high-angle view where we see the piano isolated on the beach as waves come crashing toward it. This shot begins behind Ada's shoulder as she gazes down onto her piano. But immediately a slow zoom moves past her to focus on the piano, although the view is blurred from moment to moment by the diaphanous wafting of Ada's bonnet ribbon over the foreground of the frame. We then cut to Ada's face in close-up, with the background blurred to a soft focus, as the camera begins to glide slowly around her (see colour section, between pp.90–1). Critic (and film-maker) Laleen Jayamanne's comments on the scene well suggest the emotional resonances such imagery can have for the spectator:

> The way in which the piano is performed both by Ada and by the film's *mise-en-scène* activates visual, tactile, kinaesthetic, auditory and even olfactory memory traces for the characters (the piano tuner smells the sea on it). It is therefore a multi-sensory object, and for Ada, a prosthetic extension of her body, so to speak. There are many examples of this link that people have noted, but the one I find most memorable is the two-shot of Ada gazing from a high cliff at her abandoned piano lying far below on the beach (seen in extreme long shot). A fragile (out of focus) and yet insistent jagged febrile Gothic line created by the fluttering ribbon of her bonnet seems to touch the piano (across a vast space) creating a tactile link between her body and the object of desire, enchantment and longing.[5]

It is important to the depiction of romantic longing that at this moment in the film, the link to the piano can only be at a distance and involves therefore the pain of separation. Indeed, the next shot in the sequence is a long shot of Ada from the side looking down from the cliff, but with her daughter Flora beside her and a procession of Maori leading the way from the cliff to the path away from the beach. No longer allowed her private moment, she is pulled away from her personal and exclusive bond with the piano. This static image gives way to one of intense motion: with crescendos of music, the camera swoops forward over a thick jungle rendered in eerie green as an other-worldly place. (Speaking of the film's often-unreal imagery cinematographer Stuart Dryburgh says that 'Part of the director's brief was that we would echo the film's element of underwater in the bush. "Bottom of the fish tank" was the description we used for ourselves to help define what we were looking for. So we played it murky blue-green.')[6] From this soaring shot, the scene cuts to a close-up of the feet of the procession stomping through the muck of mud that threatens to trap them in place.

The second scene of longing for the piano occurs soon after. It is so short it might not seem to count as a veritable sequence, yet it is presented as a unified moment where again looking and longing are merged. Ada returns from the wedding photo session, a dismal affair in the rain, into the house and angrily and energetically pulls off her wedding dress. As two women look on astonished, Ada goes to the window and gazes out. A reverse shot shows Ada through the window, her face softened and blurred by the streaks of rain across the glass of the window (see colour section, between pp.90–1). There is a cut to the piano back on the beach, viewed straight on with waves crashing around it and its 'feet' immersed in the water.

In the third sequence, it is the longing of Baines (Harvey Keitel) and not that of Ada that is in question. Ada has just played for Baines and the camera has swirled around as he moves in captivation from behind her to stand in front of her and look at her directly seated at the piano. From this interaction of two people that is mediated by music, the piano-playing continues across a cut into a shot of Baines lying in his bed and looking out from behind a scrim-like curtain. Although the continuation of the music across the cut suggests at first a unity of action (Baines looking at Ada?), it becomes clear with one more cut that this is a later time as a reverse-cut through the scrim (which Baines pulls aside and then lets loose again) reveals the piano alone in the frame, light streaming down around it and catching the gentle play of dust motes. The music fades away as a final shot shows Baines taking off his long shirt, standing there in the nude, moving around the piano and dusting it with his clothes in long, languorous caresses rich in ecstatic sensuality.

There is a narrative to these sequences – a dramatic movement in each sequence but also in both the progression between them and their place within the overall movement of the film – a narrative of longing and desire, of desire for objects but also for qualities beyond inanimate worldly things. Initially, the romantic film is caught in a tension between longing and its frustration, and between worldliness and utopian flight. The world is indeed at first glance the locus of frustration: against what novelist Milan

Kundera termed 'the unbearable lightness of being', worldliness asserts itself as a weighty physicality that pulls down aspiration, that works to block the realisation of dream and desire. It is important to the establishing of an initial gap between desire and fulfilment that the first segment I described tears Ada from her bonding through sight with her piano to force her on a journey that ends in the viscous bog around Stewart's house (the same dismal bog into which she will sink slowly, her dress billowing up around her, when towards the end of the film Stewart cuts her finger off upon learning of her infidelity with Baines). Worldliness is here an intensely visceral physicality, an entrapping muckiness that thwarts spirit.

But the lightness of being can't be held back, and romantic longing sets out to surpass the weighty world's hold over it. Hence, the freedom and free-floating ebullience in the romantic film of lushly graceful camera movements that liberate space (one of the top directors of the woman's film, Max Ophuls, is also one of the legendary practitioners of the gliding camera). In *The Piano*, the camera is endlessly in motion as it depicts Ada, swirling around her, creating complex arabesques that transform the world into a potential transcendence, that use the camera to choreograph life as energy and uplift.

This mutability through motion blends with another technique for the world's de-realisation: namely, a transformation of that world into something insubstantial, ethereal, the world as a nothing that has no invincible hold over its inhabitants. *The Piano* announces such de-realisation even in its very first shot: with a blurriness that almost becomes abstract, shapes beyond which we can vaguely sense a wall seem to dance delicately across the screen, creating kaleidoscopic plays of soft light; only a reverse-shot clarifies that what we have been looking at are Ada's hands held up to her eyes in a game of seeing/not-seeing.

Romantic cinema is in this fashion a cinema of soft focus, of visual blurs (as in the rain on the window), of soft wafts of light swirling down through obscurity and creating delicate patterns of glowing well-being, of an airy goldness that suffuses the image. Much of the appeal of romantic imagery, I would contend, comes from the ways it takes the edges off a hard, harsh world and substitutes a dreamy haziness in which longings and the imagining that things could be different can take flight. In terms of the woman's film, this is often the replacement of the difficult realities of the restrictions upon and violence of women's lives with a belief in the primacy of romantic love and the softness to transcend that pain and frustration. This romantic promise through a softening of the world is well captured in the Henry James novel *The Portrait of a Lady* (later, of course, to be adapted as a Jane Campion film) when Gilbert Osmond promises Isabel Archer that their marriage will be a wondrous, ethereal thing:

> My dear girl, I can't tell you how life seems to stretch there before us – what a long summer afternoon awaits us. It's the latter half of an Italian day – with a golden haze, and the shadows just lengthening, and that divine delicacy in the light, the air, the landscape, which I have loved all my life and which you love to-day. Upon my honour, I don't see why we shouldn't get on. We've got what we like – to say nothing of having each other. ... It's all soft and mellow – it has the Italian colouring.[7]

Interestingly, the floating glide of the camera and this de-realising ethereality in the imagery connect up to a third challenge to the weightiness of the world: a vibrant, sensuous tactility. This might appear paradoxical since we have just been asserting that the romantic film figures a movement away from the physical. But part of the project of the romantic film is to show how desire can take the deadly burdensomeness of the weighty world and find other realities of spirit, higher or deeper, within it (and not only outside of it in some utopian realm of yearning). The world itself, even in its physicality, is seen to harbour romantic resonance. There is the entrapping muck of the bog, but there is also the quite different physicality of a languorous touch, a gliding caress (for instance, Baines's hand sweeping along the top of the piano), a gentle probing of fingers. Indeed, if *The Piano* is filled with visceral images of primal elements that reiterate our ultimately physical nature (this is a film of puke, of blood, of dog's saliva, of mud and muck), there is also proposed in the film an alternate and uplifting physical universe of luminescent skin, of delicate touch, of clothing material wafting as it moves (like the wafting bonnet ribbon), of the feel of water as one's hands glide through it. Revealingly, even the book of the screenplay for *The Piano* has a kind of de-realising and etherealising nostalgia to it: printed in a Victorian-like sepia tone, with hazy photographs dotting the text, the book comes off less as a record of the film than as a delicate romantic object in its own right.

In the film's tension between a visceral physicality that is rendered as entrapment and a sensuous tactility that figures a soaring liberation and transcendence, *The Piano* often seems to many spectators to approach the dimension of myth. There is something quite elemental in the film in its

Primal elements

fascination with basic forms of matter – arabesques of hands in the water and crashes of waves, the omnipresence of both a natural order (the undergrowth of the forest) and of a disordered nature (as in the burnt and stunted tree trunks and messily gnarled vines around Stewart's house), swirls of light, viscous bogs, bodily secretion, a reduction of the visual look in many scenes to a primal colour that spreads over the frame (see colour section, between pp.90–1). (Likewise, some commentators have seen a primal concern with the elements in *Holy Smoke*'s recurrent images of fire, as for instance in the flickering flame of a match that fills up the frame and through which we see Ruth [Kate Winslet] looking on captivated.)

Even as it thrusts the viewer into an intensely present and physicalised world (represented in the shock cut to the mud and to the revelation of Stewart's homestead as a veritable wasteland), a world given precise place and time, the film also serves for some of its proponents as a hint at a timelessness of deeper meanings and resonances, an archetypal universe of fundamental values. Predictably, *The Piano* has been the object of Jungian analysis,[8] but revealingly, a number of the specifically feminist defences of the film also take up a position that sets out to pinpoint and valorise the seemingly mythic qualities of woman's identity and desire in opposition to dominant values of constraint and confinement for women. Hence, the reference in several analyses of *The Piano* to what has been called a French feminism – represented by Luce Irigaray and Julia Kristeva – that sees women as inhabiting a special and irreducible realm of affect and eros.

A short analysis of *The Piano* by philosophy professor Cynthia Kaufman offers a concise representation of the application of this form of feminism to the film:

> There is a rhetoric of purity in the film that bears a strong resemblance to the politics embodied in some of the French feminists. ... In *Desire in Language*, Julia Kristeva argues that a realm of feminine truth exists outside the world of male-dominated politics. The realm of the feminine and of female liberation is outside language; it exists in an uncompromised field of emotions. ... Ada exhibits Kristeva's feminine resistance by not speaking the language of the father. Her refusal to speak is presented as the ultimate act of resistance.[9]

The virtually mythic concern with an erotics of tactility helps explain the recurrence of two often-interconnected techniques in romantic cinema: an emphasis on close-ups and a fascination with hands. The hand reaches out, literally longs for connection. And as one of the primary points for the body to make tactile contact with others, it becomes a privileged figure for the realisation of romantic wish. At many moments in *The Piano*, we are offered soft close-ups of Ada's hands reaching to the keys of her piano (sometimes through the impediment of slats that the piano is boarded up within) but no image perhaps incarnates for many spectators the affective eroticism of *The Piano* more than an extreme close-up of Baines's finger lightly passing through a small tear in Ada's clothes to touch her flesh with a caress that is simultaneously timid and bold (see colour section, between pp.90–1). This is an image that is endlessly invoked and evoked in writings on *The Piano*, as if the image had etched itself inescapably into the emotions.

Romance is not only a longing for a specific thing – a person, an object like a piano – but for a promise of spirituality or radiant uplift that unity with that thing ostensibly will provide. Romance involves a sensuous tactility but it also hints at an ineffable reward beyond the merely physical. And in this respect, the cinematic cut can serve an eminently romantic function, setting up a logic of higher unity between the one who longs and the things longed for, even if they are physically separated. Take, for instance, the second of the three sequences of longing for the piano. If, in the first, Ada had looked down from the cliff at her piano with everything reiterating just how separated she is from it at this moment, the second sequence gives a transcendental power to Ada's look, one that enables the piano to be brought back into her orbit even though it is not physically present to her. Against the all too physical world immediately around her – the rain, the mud, the dismal fact of marriage, the entrapment in a house with old biddies prattling on around her – the cut offers an imaginative transport that overcomes barriers of space and time. (Frequently, romantic cinema imagines longing as a spirituality that surpasses ordinary physical laws. In Frank Borzage's classic silent film *Seventh Heaven* [1927], for instance, two lovers are physically separated by war, but are able to overcome disconnection by a veritable telepathy in which each thinks of the other, every night at the same time.)

At the end of *The Piano*, Ada rejects her fetish-object of the piano (although she almost drowns with it and risks being caught with it in the watery grave of the sea) and chooses another path for the realisation of desire (a controversial ending that has her in a domestic partnership with Baines). If romantic cinema centres on a tension between longing and the entrapping pull of a crassly visceral world, it is also the case that longing itself can become a form of entrapment, the all-consuming unity between the one who longs and the things longed for turning into a claustrophobic obsessiveness that refuses to deal with the everyday world and is frequently thereby crushed by it. If the romantic story is progressive – imagining a future that must be better, deeper, richer, than the givens of the physical present – it also flirts with the regressive, with a nostalgic longing that pulls one back towards the romantic riches one once had (or imagines were had).

The romantic film moves forward, narrates a progress in which dreams strive for fruition and fulfilment, but it is also haunted by cyclicity, by the obsessive return of the dreamer to past accomplishments, past bounties (whether actual or imagined).[10] Thus, for instance, in Ophuls's *Letter from an Unknown Woman* (1948), Lina (Joan Fontaine) turns her love for Stefan (Louis Jourdan) into a veritable regression in which she can think only of him, remember only him, and only in the glorious image she has constructed and maintained of him – a regression that renders her as a veritable child unable to survive in an adult world of forward-moving time and responsibility.[11] Films of woman's desire easily can tip over into a cinema of melodrama and madness (for example, the obsessed Alex (Glenn Close) of *Fatal Attraction* [1987]) that represents the genre's outer limits, the fatalism it constantly risks falling into. The temptation in fatal melodrama is to render the woman's primal fixations, her primary obsessions, less as the fundamental realisation of her desire than as a stunted, regressive and repressive manifestation of the very blockage of a free expression of true desire.

Ultimately trading melodrama for romance, *The Piano* tells, in fact, not only of a woman's primal bonds (her daughter, her piano, her own image as when she kisses herself in a mirror) but also narrates a process, one represented as a growth in which new and more appropriate forms and objects of desire can appear. Ada learns to break with her piano, to sever her own infantile connections to her daughter, to substitute erotic connection with another person (Baines) for other forms of attachment.

Initially, Baines's own negotiations to gain the piano and through it to capture Ada can seem like further forms of other men's domination of her (her father, her husband). Indeed, Baines's machinations to possess Ada have led some critics of the film to see its narrative, as we'll see later on, as one more rendition of women desiring their own domination. But for many defenders of the film, including some feminists, Ada's place and power in relation to the narrative of her life in New Zealand is also about her increasing assumption of control over her fate and a concomitant weakening of that masculine power that had assumed it could decide matters for her.

To a large degree, *The Piano* is in the specific tradition of the woman's film that scholars have come to term 'the woman's Gothic'. The form developed from eighteenth- and nineteenth-century literary forms (for example, *Jane Eyre* might be seen as an important antecedent of the films). In the classic tales of this tradition, which flourished in the USA and Britain in the 1940s (for example, in films like *Rebecca* [1941], *Suspicion* [1941], *Gaslight* [British version in 1940; Hollywood version in 1944], *Dragonwyck* [1946] and so on), a simple woman, often from a modest class background, finds the cyclical regularity of her limited lifestyle transformed when a stranger comes brusquely into her life, marries her and spirits her away to a wild abode away from civilisation where she is trapped and where she begins to suspect that he hates her or even has murderous designs on her.

The woman's Gothic is not so much an indigenous form as a narrative structure whose appeal can be actualised in various cultural contexts and historical moments. It flourished, for instance in the USA in the 1940s, in part because new conditions in marital relations brought about by the war uncovered suspicions about the stability and security of male–female relations. And in the 1980s and 1990s, alongside a feminism of self-empowerment (sometimes to the point of separatism), there arises a new feminism, sometimes tipping into post-feminism, in which the need for women specifically is to achieve erotic fulfilment in the heterosexual realm (this is the moment of a pro-pornography feminism, for instance). In such a moment, *The Piano* gains strong cultural resonance. By finding local means to inflect the richly affective form of the Gothic, antipodean cinema finds one way to tap into a global film market. Indeed, in a study of Australian and New Zealand cinema, *Girl's Own Stories: Australian and New Zealand Women's Films* (whose very title is a reference to a Jane Campion film), Jocelyn Robson and Beverly Zalcock examine how an earlier resonant work, Gillian Armstrong's *My Brilliant Career* (1979), sets a model for regional effort to break into an international market by offering a regional recoding of the classic woman's film:

> [I]t is classic Hollywood melodrama of the 1930s and 1940s that shapes it [*My Brilliant Career*] discursively. It is not unusual to find the films of the New Australian Cinema adopting the generic conventions of commercial Hollywood movies. Australia's national cinema, in its 1970s incarnation, had to address the twin demands of a 'quality' cinema that would deal with specifically Australian themes and the commercial requirement that the films do well internationally. As a result, the films of this period are balanced between 'art-house' and commercial – a familiar dilemma for many national cinemas. In this case, what tends to happen is the grafting of specifically Australian stories onto popular generic structures, albeit adapted and modified to some degree.[12]

To be sure, *My Brilliant Career* offers a very different trajectory for its heroine than does *The Piano* – in the earlier film, she goes off on her own at the end, independent of a man – and in the difference might lie the distance from the 1970s to 1990s. This is where the reinvigoration of the Gothic tradition in *The Piano* comes into play.

There are two variants on the woman's Gothic tradition of a wife who discovers potential threat in the mysterious man who has become her husband. In the first, there is no other significant man around, and in this case the woman usually discovers that her husband's supposed hatred and violence was really a form of love that couldn't express itself properly (the key works here are Hitchcock's *Rebecca* and *Suspicion*). In some cases within this variant, the man must go through a process of self-education in which he comes to learn how to love a woman (see, for instance, Hitchcock's *Spellbound* [1945] or Fritz Lang's *Secret Beyond the Door* [1948] where psychologically disturbed men come close to killing a woman they are in love with and have to grow out of their psychosis). In the second variant, there is a second man who contrasts with the husband, the husband is fully guilty of violence and hatred, and the woman is able to transfer her affection onto the other man (and, in many cases, be saved by him). In both versions of the Gothic film, a contrast is established between two versions of masculinity – one that is potentially dangerous and one that is loving – and the difference between the versions has to do with whether or not these polarities exist in one man (the first version in which danger must transform into love) or in two (the second variation where each man fully embodies the alternatives).

Significantly, within the Hollywood system, the traditional Gothic films often represent the other man – the saviour/rival-to-the-husband – as not at all an exotic, erotic, sensual male but as someone as ordinary as the heroine was before she married (in several cases, the other man was played by Bob Cummings, a paragon of American blandness). In this way, the traditional Gothic films often engage in a sexually conservative project in which a woman discovers that she should have been satisfied with an ordinary life with little eros or excitement and not have ventured out into a seductive and exotic realm of sexual self-expression. In contrast, *The Piano* chronicles an opening up into the realm of the erotic, and in this respect again it taps into a historical moment in which eros, desire and the body all become objects of affirmation.

In this respect, *The Piano* is closest perhaps to a sub-genre of the tradition that I have analysed elsewhere as the 'reverse Gothic': in this manifestation of the genre, the man the woman finds herself married to reveals himself to be not exotic at all but in fact inadequate in the expression of love and sensuality (in some cases, he is directly bland and boring, with no spark of sexual excitement) and the abode he takes her away to has nothing of the intriguingly exotic about it (unlike, say, Manderlay or Dragonwyck) but is a dismal, grey site where passion can take no sustenance.[13] In the 'reverse Gothic', then, it is the other man, the rival, who offers the thrills of love that the heroine cannot find in marriage, and in this way reverse Gothic films can be seen to engage in a certain critique of marriage – in its ostensible stifling of passion – even as they endorse an image of the proper heterosexual couple. A number of such films appear at the end of the 1940s in postwar America, perhaps responding to women's discontent with the mainstream ideology of matrimony in the age of the Kinsey report, of budding feminism, of fissures in the middle-class and suburban dreams of the normal family. This is the moment, for example, of the MGM adaptation of *Madame Bovary* (1949) which is explicitly about the suffocating confines of the home for the romantic woman. The reverse Gothic invests in a postwar valorisation of erotic expression that ultimately can find new resonance in the moment of the 1990s with its complicated blend of feminism and post-feminism, and the emotional investment in narratives that separate a repressive masculinity from a supposedly more sensitive, caring one.

Here, we can begin to see the importance of Baines for the erotic effect of *The Piano*. If in the first variant of the Gothic film, the husband himself can learn, or be taught by the woman, to temper his violence (and the insecurity that fuels it) with love and sharing (as in Hitchcock's *Suspicion*), in the second version, there is no erotic hope for the husband and the woman must find passion elsewhere, in the arms of another man (and in the reverse Gothic, he is presented as much more passionate than the affectless husband). Many fans of *The Piano* attest to the extreme charm

Gothic entrapment

The feminised Baines

and erotic charge they receive from the image of Baines as the other man in Ada's life. The film even toys with the audience in this respect in the sequence of Baines in the nude dusting the piano. As he moves around it, the image offers a veritable game of hide-and-seek with his penis, playing with the viewer's desire to see. In contrast, in the previous year's *Bad Lieutenant* (1992), Keitel had an even more revealing scene of frontal nudity, but there it expressed an unerotic descent into self-degradation on the part of his character. Indeed, even though he had been around in cinema for many years, *The Piano* transformed the somewhat chunky (and, in many films, sleazy or decadent) Harvey Keitel into a veritable sex symbol.

Baines is shown to possess a degree of sensitivity to women that is just waiting to flower. It is not that he is not initially dominated by a brutishness, but within the toughened exterior of this man who has obviously seen some of the roughness of life, there is a glimpse of something else, a sensitivity. In this respect, Baines finds his place in the long cinematic (and literary) tradition of rough men who are revealed to have a softness underneath.

The importance of the sequence I cited earlier of Baines staring at the piano he has acquired becomes clear. The man has become caught up in the intense circuits of passion that involve Ada and her piano and that he wants to participate in, whether out of desire or of envy. When Baines looks out through the scrim at the piano, he is lying in bed almost as if he were sick or stricken, reflecting or even moping, and there is much about the short sequence that suggests that the enigma – of music and the aesthetic dimension, of femininity – has put Baines into a passive, dependent position. It is a position, we might say, that approximates stereotypes of romantic femininity: the passive supineness; the etherealising of the surroundings by the evanescent flimsiness of the scrim; the soft light playing down over the dust motes; the lush music that plays over this scene from the previous one and suggests that Baines's brooding passivity is a consequence of the active efforts of Ada's piano playing; the narratively extraneous movement of the camera that reveals no new information, but that in gliding behind the scrim, emphasises a softening of focus (like the fingers that move back and forth across the face in the first shot) and has a quality of ineffable stylistic flourish (like the winding camera in Ophuls).

In Campion's subsequent films of romantic heterosexuality, male figures also pass through a process of feminisation that gives their masculinity a sensitive core (although, as we'll see in a later section, there is much about their depiction that ultimately blocks romantic investment – whether by the female protagonist or by the affectively inclined spectator). In *The Portrait of a Lady*, for instance, the refinements of an elegant way of life lead many of the men to come off as veritable dandies (for example, Gilbert Osmond) and Isabel's refusal of the amorous intents of several of her suitors puts them, rather than her, in the passive position of obsession. Like the woman in the romance narrative, the male figure here loses a forward-progressing activeness to fall into a cyclicity of captivation, as in the case of Lord Warburton who never gets over Isabel and keeps coming back to her (in a revealing omission, the film does not include the novel's late announcement that Lord Warburton has finally found a British society woman to transfer his affections onto). And it is evident that the fatally ill Ralph Touchett is, in his malady and the repose and effortlessness it necessitates, placed in a position of moping passivity, one that is only intensified by his own obsessive love for Isabel.

Holy Smoke takes the feminisation of the man even further as Ruth puts a dress on P. J. (Harvey Keitel), applies lipstick to his mouth and ties up his hair with a bow. For a long stretch of the film, P. J. will remain in this garb, running helplessly after Ruth with agonised declarations of love. Interestingly, Campion seems to have incorporated cross-dressing into the very work of film production in ways that play with traditional images of masculinity, as Claire Corbett, the assistant editor for *The Piano* recounts in a production diary:

> Photographs from the shoot [of *The Piano*] in New Zealand line the walls of the cutting rooms: photos of the actors in costume, of the crew, of Harvey Keitel in a dress. Jane Campion always has a dress day at least once during her shoots; all cast and crew have to wear dresses. The men love it. The most macho change their dresses several times a day. Often the women find it more traumatic. Jane says she feels much closer to her male crew members once she's seen them in a dress.[14]

As films of the 1990s, whatever the time-frame within their narrative world, Campion's last three films are very much of a cultural moment hovering between feminism and post-feminism and caught up in many cases in an effort to redeem men or at least to find mitigating circumstances for their inadequacies (one signpost of the age is 1999's *Stiffed: The Betrayal of the American Man* by feminist author Susan Faludi; for Faludi, there are structural failures in the postwar economic system of the American dream that betrayed frequently well-meaning men).[15] Where the Reagan–Bush years had witnessed a cinematic fascination with what some commentators referred to as a 're-masculinisation' incarnated in extreme form in bulging muscle action heroes (Schwarzenegger, Van Damme, Bruce Willis in the *Die Hard* trilogy), there is in the 1990s especially an insistence on valorising a masculinity that is sensitive, caring and that can be sympathetic to the needs of women even as it maintains a belief in the seductive potency of masculinity. 'Hey, straight boys! Are you gay enough?' asks the title of an article in *Talk Magazine* which discusses the attractiveness to urban professional women of men who are soft and gentle and yet never allow this to diminish their unwavering heterosexuality.

At the same time, there has been significant controversy over *The Piano*'s depiction of Baines's negotiations with Ada, in which he gains sexual favours in exchange for piano keys. For some, Baines's actions resemble nothing so much as a form of sexual blackmail, one that men, as the holders of power, frequently wield. Take, for instance, Tania Modleski's response to a *Village Voice* review by Georgia Brown that praises Baines as being 'like the wise tamer in horse movies: patient, attuned to the animal, instinctively sensing when a direct move might be made': as Modleski replies,

> An arrangement that makes the woman into (something resembling) a horse before it makes her a whore would seem to me to be rather exploitative all along – to say nothing of the fact that it is the man, not the woman, who recognises this exploitation when it is finally noticed. Brown's language reveals the extent to which the heroine lacks agency and is testimony to the fact that women continue to experience their dehumanisation as erotic.[16]

The Piano depicts a situation in which economic possession intertwines with the possession of women. But for those to whom *The Piano* incarnates romantic fantasy in a positive fashion, the point of the film's depiction of the ways Baines connects ownership of the piano to sexual control is that even in this realm where the man is assumed to be in power, the vulnerability of masculinity can eventually become manifest. Baines is a sort of entrepreneur who discovers that the market has mysteries beyond his control and that he is an object as much as an agent of barter. Naomi Segal's discussion of Baines offers a representative example of an approach that defends *The Piano*'s sexual politics as feminist insofar as it narrates a woman's coming to power in sexual and economic arenas that have excluded her as anything other than an object of desire and exchange:

> Colonisation comes from and operates by the structures of capitalism: grading, marking and counting out. Analogous to piano keys and fingers, numbered territorial stakes measure out the landscape and buttons are supposed to pay for it. These are Stewart's coinage. Baines and Ada begin with black and white keys, black overclothes and white underclothes; but at a certain moment, the bargaining stops and with it the grading of access which is undoubtedly one

> mode of the erotic, creating an appetite in both the heroine and the audience. Baines is after all, like the husband, a colonial exploiter, but less absolutely, not so much an owner as a mediator and interpreter. Implicated nonetheless, he buys the piano and expects to buy Ada; but let us not forget that Ada is as hard a bargainer as he is and it is he who stops the negotiation first.[17]

Note that Segal's comments commence with a recognition of men's possessiveness: it is typical of the approach that sees *The Piano* in a positive light as redeeming the male that it starts by admitting the propensity of men for domination, but then narrates a potential for changeability in *some* men. In this respect, it is necessary to note that the passage from Segal also makes a distinction between Baines and Stewart (the quality of the 'less absolutely' that separates the former from colonial rapaciousness) and redeems one in contrast to the other.

Some defenders of *The Piano*'s depiction of Baines operate, then, by cataloguing a series of traits that separate him off from Stewart. On the one hand, Stewart appears as the incarnation of rapacious entrepreneurial possessiveness. He is associated with a drive for ownership and for a conversion of the natural into the personally owned (if the area around his house is so scarred and desolate, this is because he has been engaging in a slash-and-burn assault on the forest). Literary theorist Carol Jacobs sums up this image of Stewart:

> When he is not buying land or burning it back he splits fence posts, marks them with his initials and small blood-red ribbons, and drives them into the ground to mark the border of his possessions. It makes perfect sense, therefore, that later in the film, to contain the passions of his wife whom he has discovered with Baines, he nails planks he has hewn to window and door to secure the boundary of his marital chattel.[18]

When Stewart discovers Ada's love note to Baines written on a piano key, he resorts to hideous violence, using the same axe to chop off her finger – to both mutilate her and to silence her hands that speak through the piano.

From the first time he sees Ada play on the beach, Baines senses a deeper poetry of life even if his social-sexual origins have not fully pre-

Slash and burn

pared him in the ways to enable that poetry. As many commentators note, Baines seems to exist between the world of the coloniser and the colonised and not to easily take up a position in one or the other camp: with half-finished Maori tattoos, with knowledge of the Maori language and their customs (and perhaps, it is implied, with sexual relations with some of their women), with a certain unsocial isolation from other white settlers (Baines is evidently a loner), Baines appears to many viewers to take up a distance, a difference, from a pure will to domination.

In offering an enumeration of primary elements of *The Piano* that derive from the classic tradition of the woman's film/romantic film and that may account for much of its affective pull, I need to note that to say there is a certain historical tradition that we can analyse as the 'woman's film' is not to assume that this is the only cinema that can or should appeal to women. We might note, for instance, how feminist critic Laura Mulvey called for a new woman's cinema that would not be in thrall to affect and visual pleasure. Referring to what she approves of as the 'first blow taken against the monolithic accumulation of traditional film conventions (already undertaken by radical film-makers)', Mulvey suggests that such a blow 'destroys the satisfaction, pleasure and privilege of the "the invisible guest" [i.e. the typical cinematic spectator who goes to the cinema for visual pleasure]'. But she argues that such an attack on pleasure is not to be regretted: 'Women, whose image has continually been stolen and used for this end, cannot view the decline of the traditional film form with anything more than sentimental regret.'[19] In other words, Mulvey posits that there can be a new cinema specifically for women, one that emphatically rejects prior modes of appealing to female spectators (note, for instance, that a bonding with traditional film form is associated with the 'sentimental').

We need then to note the range of possible positions on woman's desire and woman's cinema and to suggest that for many spectators *The Piano* is an extreme incarnation – for better or worse – of one or another of these positions. On the one hand, the film has been applauded for offering women a place where sentiment can gain full expression. The film has also been condemned for remaining at the level of sentiment and romantic escapism and for using these to excuse male domination. And, interestingly, a third affirming approach uses Mulvey's approach to argue that *The Piano* actually participates in the elaboration of a new woman's cinema that is not in fact in thrall to dominant cinematic pleasure. In other words, for some commentators, the film becomes a positive embodiment of a 'Mulveyan' cinema. For example, with explicit reference to Mulvey, feminist critic Stella Bruzzi contends that *The Piano* breaks from standard representations of the feminine as the objectified target of a male gaze and is connected to 'a complex feminist displacement of the conventionalised objectification of the woman's form'.[20] Contrasting *The Piano* to traditional costume films, such as *Picnic at Hanging Rock* (1975) or *The Age of Innocence* (1993), Bruzzi argues that in the latter works, 'The act of looking is closely affiliated with men and the expression of masculine sexuality, and in these costume films a class-heterosexual dynamic has been constructed whereby the women are defined and confined by their "to-be-looked-at-ness"' (a term directly from Mulvey). In contrast, '*The Piano*, enforcing a simple inversion of the normative process addresses the question of what happens when the agent of the gaze is female and its object is the male body.'[21] (See colour section, between pp.90–1.)

It is also necessary to note that there has been much debate around the film's depiction of the Maori people. For instance, in an oft-cited short piece on the film, Maori critic Leonie Pihama argues that the film's marginalisation and stereotyping offers little pleasure to Maori women. For Pihama, the Maori characters are used in the film in ways that deprive them of agency and turn them instead into symbols – whether of a mythic realm that European entrepreneurial culture cannot understand (as is the case with Stewart) or of a primitive way of life that white femininity must ultimately distance itself from.[22] Literature professor Anna Neill gives a good summary of this critique in her essay on the New Zealand context of the film's story:

> [W]hile the Maori may not exactly be relegated to nature, they do not inhabit anything like a contemporary historical space within the colonising culture. They alternate between childlike fascination with, and a terror of the mysterious objects that the Europeans fetishise (a fascination and a terror which are shared to some extent by the childish, scatter-brained Scots character Nessie). ... Scenes of contact are limited to these moments of cultural inscrutability, stripped of any sense of political conflict. ... [Q]uestions of culture are de-politicised and the Maori become frozen in time.[23]

Sharp examination of the representation of the Maori has been central to a critical analysis that wants to examine issues of gender and race together. Earlier I quoted Cynthia Kaufman writing of the ties of *The Piano* to the French feminism of writers like Julia Kristeva, who valorise a special realm in which women's desires ostensibly can emerge and find expression. But it is important to note that where many feminists who adhere to a politics of erotics and personal desire find *The Piano* virtually embodies this politics in its look and feel, Kaufman ultimately argues that the political promotion of pleasure has itself to be interrogated politically: who is the pleasure for? at whose expense? In particular, Kaufman argues that the film needs to turn the Maori people into mythic and agency-less figures in order to demarcate Ada's struggle for self-expression from the world around her. For Kaufman, it is *The Piano*'s very creation of a mythic image of 'woman' that has invited and indeed requires critique – and this from a position that rightfully qualifies as feminist – as a film that universalises on the basis of only one version of femininity and feminine desire – a white heterosexual one. Kaufman herself suggests that the film builds up its image of the desiring and self-expressive white woman at the expense of Maori people in the film.

Kaufman notes, for instance, that one of the actions that early on establishes Ada's determination is her insistence that Stewart have her piano transported back to the homestead from the beach. Explicitly, this scene is presented as a racially uninflected clash of masculine and feminine wills – and thus could be seen as representing the quest of feminine desire for expression – but implicitly, as Kaufman argues, it is also about exploitation of indigenous people by the whites since they are the ones who will have to do the gruelling work of transport for Ada's benefit. As Kaufman puts it,

> Some white men need to muck around with the natives, but to the extent that they can protect their women from work and nature, they are in touch with the sublime. The men do the dirty work of colonialism while the women stay clean. White women are constructed as pure to offer white society as a whole a conception of itself as superior through its separation from nature.[24]

In fact, Kaufman goes even further in taking a distance from Kristeva to posit that the stereotyping of the Maori people is concomitant with a stereotyping of Ada as white woman. For Kaufman, there is a curious shift in the film by which the Kristevan association of woman with a natural force

Maori people as backdrop

of desire is displaced into the assumption that Ada needs to grow up by leaving the mucky natural world behind for the purity and cleanliness of the white-dominated city (the images at the end of the film of Ada, Baines and Flora safely domiciled in the town of Nelson). In other words, Ada may represent a primal force of feminine desire and expression, but these qualities are presented by the film as something other than primitive, as something indeed that needs to go beyond primitive roots to achieve its full fruition. As Kaufman puts it,

> Out of nature, they [Ada, Baines and Flora] are in the tame world of European culture, bathed in white light and flooded with Western classical music. ... Baines lives with Ada and Flora in a clean world, safe from the mud and terror that existed in the heart of darkness in the jungle. Money and resources come to the civilised world without the need for direct personal compromise.[25]

Kaufman offers a conclusion that seems directly to assail the mythic position that concentrates on the individual (white) woman's struggle of desire and expression:

> If Ada is read simply as a victorious feminist heroine who achieves liberation through a tactic of silent resistance – and when the goal of that liberation is purity – we have a feminism that reinforces white privilege and that robs itself of political efficacy.... Much of *The Piano*'s appeal rests in its promise of white female liberation existing comfortably within the structures of colonial domination.[26]

I will return shortly to the debate and disagreement about *The Piano*. For the moment, though, I want to linger on the affirmative response to the film while keeping in mind the possible incompleteness of that response across the range of viewers. In this respect, we might note how objections to the film – to its sexual or racial politics, for example – can become further incitations on the part of lovers of the film to intensify and fortify their love. So strong can bonding with *The Piano* be that critiques of the film are taken to be veritable challenges to the personhood of the spectator, and this leads to even more intense investment in the film. That is, the defenders are also forced into close analysis. But the goal of this analysis is to find elements that confirm the film's qualities. To take just one example, note the response made by some proponents of *The Piano* to critiques that have attacked the narrative finale of the film – in which Ada suddenly fights against a possibly self-willed death by drowning, rises to the surface and then ends up happily in middle-class domestic bliss with Baines and a new piano – for its ostensible suggestion that settling down is the appropriate culmination of feminine desire. Against this critique of the film's domesticating project, some ardent defenders of *The Piano* opt for a reading – rather than just a fully anti-analytic ineffable appreciation – based on a focus on details of the work that they argue will support the film's feminism. In particular, the defenders note that *after* the explicit *narrative* conclusion, the film offers a non-narrative coda image: Ada's body floating in the water above her piano – an image of what would have happened if she had given in to her drowning. Ada's own voice-over at this point suggests that her consciousness lives not only in her physically present middle-class world but in a realm of imagination and nostalgia that offers her comfort: 'At night I think of my piano in its open grave and sometimes of myself floating above it. Down there everything is so still and silent that it lulls me to sleep. It is a weird lullaby and so it is; it is mine.' Sue Gillett offers a representative version of the sort of reading of this scene that defends the film against anti-feminist charges:

> The return to this second image, coming so soon after Ada's rescue from drowning, unsettles the happily-ever-after of the couple, not in that it forebodes an end to this happiness but in its recognition of the insistent presence of another territory and mode of experience. There is not so much a tension between the two images, awaiting resolution, as a balance. Ada has chosen life, and she has embraced that choice with surprised pleasure; but, as her final voiceover reminds us, accompanied as it is by a return to a now serene, soft focus image of her floating gracefully, peacefully attached to the piano-coffin by a taut rope, death still lies beneath or within this choice, has enabled this choice – is not, that is, in opposition to it.[27]

It seems inevitable in a cultural moment such as ours where there is debate and disagreement on the political implications of desire and its ties to eros and power that a film like *The Piano* would spark disagreement (and would be seen as both embodying and denying a feminist position). We might, then, provisionally conclude our analysis of the affect and effect of the film by sandwiching it between two writings on it, one responding to the other and each bearing symmetrical but contrasting titles: 'What Music Is', an ebullient ode to the film by Kerryn Goldsworthy in *Arena Magazine*, an Australian socialist journal, and 'What Rape Is', a letter-to-the-editor reply in the next issue of *Arena* by Lisa Sarmas.[28]

It is significant that Goldsworthy's high praise for the film appears in a politically committed journal, for her review is very much in tune with a radical politics that centres on women's erotic self-expression. Many of the procedures and arguments that we find in writers who admit their captivation by *The Piano* are in evidence here and in an interconnected fashion. First, there is a recourse to an autobiographical or even confessional mode (as we also saw with web fans) in which the critic searches for a personal style that seems intended both to evoke the emotionalism of the film and to enable the critic to participate poetically in the process of the film. Thus, Goldsworthy follows a discussion with the ways the piano functions for Ada as an object of desire with a personal account: in parentheses, she tells us, '(The Easter before last, I bought a piano after seventeen years without one. I sat up playing it till two or three o'clock for a week. ... I couldn't take my hands off it. I thought about it all the time)' (p. 47).

Second, the 'analysis' of the film verges on an admission that for the lover of it, this is a film that is less amenable to the dry dissections of analysis than to a description of the film's resonant evasions of the cold logic of narrative: 'The grammar of images in *The Piano* reminds you that a movie, like a sentence, is not a linear progression but a molecular structure, a precise arrangement of words and phrases or of shots and scenes that link up and lock in and loop back and will, without reference to each other, make only a mutilated kind of sense' (p. 48).

Third and consequently, the language of criticism becomes increasingly lyrical as if trying to make words replay the poetic texture and affect of the film. For instance, the final lines of Goldsworthy's review refer to such images as that oft-cited one of Baines's finger reaching through the hole in

Ada's stocking and contend that these 'open up abruptly into endless possibilities of discovery and exploration: of what the body might do, what the ocean might mean, how love might work, what music is' (p. 48). Music and desire come together in this approach as forces that are politically important because in fact they offer a flight of freedom from the sway of politics. Interestingly, Goldsworthy does have criticism of the film – namely, that the narrative of the film requires Ada to give up her piano in exchange for a love relationship. As she puts it, 'The implication is that if a woman has True Love then that ought to be enough to make her happy, and to want to be able to play the piano in that effortless, rapt transcendent way as well is just bloody unreasonable' (p. 47). Nonetheless, Goldsworthy appears to adhere to a political perspective that takes the aesthetic dimension to offer escape from crass mechanics of possession and exchange: revealingly, her critique of the film's ending occurs in a section titled 'Economics' which is then immediately followed, as if it were an answer, by a section on 'Images' that begins 'It's not just the unrelenting beauty of almost every shot that makes the visual aspect of the film extraordinary' (p. 48). Aesthetics trumps the crassly economic. From this point on, the essay offers nothing but praise for the film.

For Goldsworthy, indeed, *The Piano* is highly defensible as a film about the transcendental uplift of romance. If it is all too easy for Goldsworthy to name an explicit theme of the film – '*The Piano* is insistently a movie about exchange' – it is also all too necessary for her to suggest at the same time that there is something beyond naming, something radiantly ineffable, in the film and that this something gives the film erotic political force. Here, for instance, is Goldsworthy's evocative description of the bargain between Ada and Baines: '[T]he "things I'd like to do while you play" turn out to be imaginative, drawn-out, delicate ceremonies punctuated by moments of frightening aggression, so redolent with erotic ambivalence and threatening mystery' (p. 47).

If Goldsworthy follows the affirmative tradition in *Piano* criticism by assuming that there is so much about the film that can't be named but only felt, Lisa Sarmas in her reply fully and confidently contends that it is easy to name the film and say what it is about: rape. Quoting Goldsworthy's

Alternate endings?

description (above) of the bargain as about 'erotic ambivalence and threatening mystery', Sarmas answers emphatically and unambiguously, 'This is a particularly disturbing description of sexual assault.' Like the lovers of the film, Sarmas talks of the film's emotional resonance for her, but what she has felt affectively is disturbance. Note, for instance, the confessional aspect in Sarmas's denunciation of the film: 'The image which still haunts me is that of Baines sexually abusing Ada while she has tried to do that which she loved most. This was the ultimate betrayal.' Where Goldsworthy finds the political problems of the film redeemed by an aesthetic dimension, Sarmas sees artistry as one of the means by which a dangerous ideology makes itself palatable and even seductive: 'When rape becomes a "bargain," when it is obscured by artistic lingo, when what *rape* is, is called "what music is," films and their reviewers have a lot to answer for.'

I'd like to leave *The Piano* here between these two positions (and recognising that there are also possibilities for mediation, as when Cynthia Kaufman can invoke two feminisms *vis-à-vis* the film: on the one hand, a French feminism that valorises expressions of personal desire; on the other hand, a feminism inflected by issues of race that wonders at whose expense personal expression is enabled). I entitled this chapter 'Dividing Lines' first of all because Campion's film speaks to and from the political and socio-sexual splits of our historical moment, a complicated moment of feminism, of post-feminism, of re-masculinisation, of revision of masculinity in supposedly sensitive directions, and of the frequent blur of all of these together. The film divides spectators, pushing both its lovers and its detractors to take up relations to it that are quite emotional, quite affective.

While, as we'll see, a concentration on feminine self-determination runs through many of the films she has made, *The Piano* may stand out in its insistence on the affirmative ties of such self-determination to heterosexual romance. *The Piano* is something unique in the history of romantic representation and in the course of Campion's career. It is to the beginnings of that career that we now turn.

Four
Beginnings: Intention and Method

> I'm happy being whatever I am, marginal or ... You know, I am tired of being called, of my films being called quirky, I must say. And I think that any critic or viewer who uses the word 'quirky' in reference to anything that's like slightly left of the mainstream should be hunted down and ... I don't know what ... shipped off to Gilligan's Island forever or something. I'm starting to get ready, I don't know, to take action against the word 'quirky.'
>
> Director Jim Jarmusch in response to the question of whether or not he is tempted to go commercial[1]

Jane Campion was born in 1954 in Wellington, New Zealand, to parents from a theatrical background: her father was a director and her mother an actor.[2] (Campion's mother plays the role of a teacher in *An Angel at My Table*, and a scene in which she recites a poem and young girls imaginatively visualise what she is talking about is readable as a tribute to Jane Campion's mother's powers of captivating performance.) Campion studied anthropology at Victoria University, Wellington. Some writers on her work have tried to suggest that it was in such study that her interest in other cultures and non-mainstream forms of experience was initiated, but in interviews Campion tends to suggest that the anthropology course she was on was too oriented to structural analysis *à la* Claude Lévi-Strauss to fuel her interests in the mythological and in a romantic take on cultural diversity. Like many college students, Campion undertook a formative trip to Europe with much of the time spent in Venice and London – where she appears to have worked on television commercials and where she suggests she generally was unhappy (some commentators have tried to draw parallels between Campion's gloomy experiences in England and Italy with those of Isabel Archer in *The Portrait of a Lady*). Moving, upon her return, to Australia, Campion turned to the visual arts and did a second degree, in painting, at Sydney College of Arts. From this point on, Campion would identify herself more in Australian rather than New

Zealand terms, a shift in national allegiance that has been controversial for many commentators.

In interviews, Campion repeatedly notes that in art school she increasingly tended towards paintings and drawings that told stories or offered up mini-narrative anecdotes. She also wrote stories and began to experiment with the production of short films. Her first effort in Super-8, *Tissues*, remains a film that Campion refers to with great fondness: it recounts a story of familial molestation – thus anticipating the subject matter of works like *A Girl's Own Story* and *Sweetie* – and takes its title from the fact that tissues appear in every scene. With a growing interest in cinema as a means of visual expression, Campion applied and was accepted into the prestigious Australian School of Film, Radio and Television (AFTRS). There, she began to form friendships that also constitute the first manifestations of her recurrent desire to work with the same people on many projects: in particular, she found great companionship with Sally Bongers who would be her cinematographer on several films and who would be in large part responsible for refining the distinctive style of the early films (with *Sweetie*, Bongers would become the first woman to serve as director of photography for an Australian 35mm film), and Gerard Lee, who was Campion's boyfriend during her time at the school and collaborated on several works such as *Peel* and *Passionless Moments*. Even after their break-up, Lee would return to work with Campion as co-scriptwriter on *Sweetie* (there is some indication that Lee had a relative who inspired the character of Sweetie). In addition to the three short films produced during the time at AFTRS that would begin to garner her critical attention – *Peel*, *Passionless Moments* and *A Girl's Own Story* – Campion also directed a video work, *Mishaps: Seduction and Conquest*. In an interview, Campion says that the video experiment was

> about two brothers: one is climbing Mount Everest – that is Mallory in the 1924 expedition – and the other is his fictional brother, who is trying to seduce a woman who is not very interested in him. It is the two styles of conquest. ... I quite like the finished film. It has a nice feeling and is more sophisticated than some of my other stuff. But I hated it when I first finished it. I made it in a very open-handed way.[3]

Campion graduated from AFTRS in 1984. Interestingly, she seems to have already had ideas leading towards a production of *The Piano* (called *The Piano Lesson* in its first screenplay versions, and eventually changed when it was discovered that there was a play of that name). Early drafts of the tale appear to have ended with much more violence (more fingers cut off, Baines actually killing Stewart). Campion says in interviews that she felt she needed to mature in her film work before undertaking such an ambitious costume drama and that she needed more of a reputation in order to raise the necessary funds for such a project. Campion also toyed with a more mythological premise for a film to be called *Ebb*. She describes this unproduced project in this manner:

> It was an imaginary story about a country where one day the sea leaves to never return, and the way in which the people have to find a spiritual solution to this problem. The natural world had become artificial and unpredictable and the film spoke about faith and doubt. The inhabitants of this country had developed a certain form of spirituality, hearing voices, having visions.[4]

Interestingly, *Ebb* was supposed to include the Thomas Hood quotation that ended up as the conclusion to *The Piano*: 'There is a silence where hath been no sound. There is a silence where no sound may be in the cold grave, under the deep sea.'

Campion went to work for the Women's Film Unit of Film Australia where she made the short film *After Hours* – about sexual harassment. In interviews, Campion tends to portray the work at the Film Unit as too caught up in hierarchies and plays of power, and strictures and structures, and she did not continue with the Unit. Instead, she worked in television (including *Two Friends* and an episode of a series revolving around the world of dance, *Dancing Daze*): her producer on *Two Friends* was Jan Chapman who became another close member of Campion's cohort and would work again with her as producer.

Cannes Film Festival scout Pierre Rissient took an intense interest in Campion's early works and, while she was still a film student, arranged for her films to be shown at the 1986 festival, along with *Two Friends*. Despite some projection problems, the screenings were ultimately a success and

Campion won the prize for best short film for *Peel*. The success of the shorts enabled Campion to come up with financing for her first feature, *Sweetie*, which, once it had a secure distribution deal from Arenafilm, received development funds of AUD575,000 from the Australian Film Commission which contributed money from its Special Production Fund to help increase the film's budget. (Later on, the AFC would also contribute AUD143,000 for the script development of *The Piano*.) Rissient continued to be one of Campion's strongest advocates. He arranged for *Sweetie* to be shown in competition at the 1989 festival where, unfortunately, it met with some resistance and even anger (evidently, there were walk-outs and booing, although Rissient himself says that reports of the film's failure at Cannes were exaggerated). Rissient would also be quite instrumental later on in arranging French financing for *The Piano* and getting it shown at Cannes.[5]

The Early Shorts

At the risk of deportation to Jim Jarmusch's Gilligan gulag, I want to begin to detail Campion's early career and suggest that a defining particularity of it is precisely something that a notion of the 'quirky' well approximates. There might even be a need to defend an idea of quirkiness insofar as criticism of it can easily slide into a critique specifically of *women*'s cultural production, deemed to be given over to lightweight ephemera of everyday emotional life and thereby dismissed as trivial. Maybe the most benign way to negotiate Jarmusch's comment is to imagine some of its intent. It is perhaps not so much a specific term that Jarmusch objects to as the attitudes its most common usage implies: that is, what Jarmusch seems to be bothered by is an approach that, when faced by *anything* outside mainstream norms of cinematic entertainment, can deal with such difference only by consigning it to an unexamined realm of the curiously exotic. But this sense of the quirky as an attitude of dismissal might be different from that of deliberate attempts on the part of a film-maker him- or herself to create differences by deforming norms in strikingly evident patterns. There is in many of the early Campion films a systematically arranged 'making strange' – making strange mainstream ways of filming and of recounting a story, but also making strange non-cinematic 'normal' ways of seeing – that is often comical and even, I dare say, quirky. (Or as the summary judgment on the Internet Movie Database of *Sweetie* puts it in a three-word assessment, 'hilarious and unusual'.)

Quoting from Campion, American film critic Roger Ebert gives a succinct description of the bold evidence of *Sweetie*'s look: '"In most films," Campion says, "what people are doing is trying to pretend the shots aren't there." Campion and Bongers don't do that. All of their shots are there.'[6]

A profile by Mary Colbert (in the Australian journal *Cinema Papers*) of cinematographer Sally Bongers helps explain some of the systematic distinctiveness and even strangeness of the film's look across the range of its shots. Bongers and Campion had met, as I noted earlier, while students at the AFTRS, and appear to have shared a rebellious resistance to what they perceived as the mainstream narrative norms being taught there. Like Campion, Bongers had a strong visual sense coming from a background in art (prior to the AFTRS, she studied Art and Design at the West Australia Institute of Technology) and this encouraged her to think of ways in which the composition of the film image might lead to effects not simply narrative in nature. As Colbert explains, '[Campion and Bongers] are not interested in the big epic, but the little moments that shape lives; the interior which must be expressed through small gestures; the ordinary that becomes the extraordinary.'[7] Bongers herself claims:

> I have to be bold about what I do. I don't mean that the visual has to take over, but that it should enhance the meaning and make it stronger. Film language can express so much and I feel really driven to add that dimension. I don't believe Australian films have visually challenged audiences much in the past; the cinematography is so restrained. The camera is used in a literal way. … There seems to be little questioning of the reason for a particular shot.[8]

Colbert describes some of the specific techniques that Bongers employs:

> A favourite means of changing perspective is shooting high angles downwards. Bongers gives as an example from *Sweetie* where Kay is lying in bed after having

> observed Sweetie's washing their father in the bath. The camera and audience look down on Kay's face to register her shock and confusion. ... Not surprisingly, Bongers was inspired by such 'art' film-makers as Godard, Tarkovsky, and Antonioni, who rebelled against traditional linear formats and sought a deeper level of expression of the inner self through images. She was impressed by their unconventional way of looking at the world: their reversal of relationship between people and subjects; the depersonalised perspective, the radical use of space and time. The early films of Antonioni, especially, influenced Bongers's ideas on framing. ... 'I love setting frames [says Bongers] and working out where things should be. When I'm composing a frame, I like to start out with it empty and place things in it gradually, building up the layers till eventually it conveys everything the script requires. But it's important for me to start with that clean slate.' As much as possible, Bongers likes to create the illusion of depth by lighting deep into the frame and by choreographing the actors to and from the camera. She also loves a dark look and heaps of contrast.[9]

In many ways, it is systematic strangeness that seems to characterise the range of Campion's earliest films (Bongers does not work as director of photography on Campion films after *Sweetie* and it must be said that these later films don't have as systematically bizarre a look, and stylistic exaggeration tends increasingly to be limited to special moments in the films). To be sure, the emphasis on the bizarre doesn't drop out even with the seriousness and artistic ambition of *The Piano* with its mainstream appeal. Among other things, Ada's muteness (and later her loss of a finger) establishes her as different from those around her in a way that puts her in the company of troubled or damaged women such Kay (from *Sweetie*), Sweetie and Janet Frame. As Ada's voice-over notes at the end of the film about her life in Nelson, 'I am quite the town freak, which satisfies'. There is something of the not normal in the world of *The Piano*, a difference rendered in the narrative as a conflict of worlds and ways of life. Likewise, the film is filled with striking images that stand out by their very deliberateness (for example, the camera shot of the gigantic sea horse that Ada and Flora have fashioned out of sand and rocks on the beach).

But there's a comic weirdness to the early films that is not maintained in *The Piano*. In *The Piano*, there is little to laugh at, for instance, and little that speaks simply of a joyful playfulness about the mechanics of cinema (one small exception is the quick cutaway when Flora makes up the story of her dad dying when struck by a lightning bolt: as she describes this gruesome death, we cut to a brief cartoon image of a man going up in flames). To be sure, as we'll see, the early films do at times deal with serious issues (madness, sexual exploitation, incest, family strife) that resonate for spectators, but frequently a surreal style turns attention away from subject matter to the films' status as quirky efforts at visual experimentation through distortion.

Peel (1982)

The official title of *Peel* is *Peel: An Exercise in Discipline* but the opening titles of the film reverse main title and subtitle. We might understand this film to be about an exercise in discipline in three ways. First, within the story world of the film, characters strive for a self-discipline, a control of one's emotions in volatile situations: a brother and sister are trying not to explode – at each other and at the man's son, who is misbehaving. The adults especially try to hold their anger in but instead of this self-discipline being seen as a positive appeasement of familial tensions, it is shown (especially with the sister) to be a form of repression and alienation: with their resentment welling up inside but kept in check by passive exteriors, the characters become isolated, non-communicating figures fully given over to their separation from others.

This inadequate self-discipline parallels another mode of discipline that the film recounts: not the control one exerts over the self, but the control directed to others, the rules and pressures we work to impose on others. Most of all, the father tries to discipline his son (to pick up orange peels he has been dropping out of the car window) and then finds at the film's conclusion that he has to redirect the act of disciplining to his sister whose impatience with the family dynamic has led her to also throw peels onto the side of the road. Revealingly, towards the end of the film, the father and son appear to have reconciled, and the two of them together vociferously engage in the disciplining of the sister. 'Pick it up!' yells the young boy to his aunt, but his exhortations come to no avail, and in the last shot we see the father sunk in passivity at the unworkability of the family situation. Self-discipline is a retreat into inactivity, but the disciplining of others leads to the same outcome given the resistance of people to be moulded by the wishes of others. The opening credits of the film include a geometric image representing the family dynamic of these three people as an inverted triangle with each person at one of the poles and connected to each other by bold, direct lines. The family here is a practice of geometric discipline in which each takes up a stance and tries to make the others take up positions that will in fact shift through a range of permutations of interpersonal behaviour. In fact, in the very feel of its first images – for instance, in the shape of its title words, all in bold and angular capital letters; in a fascination with quickly glimpsed lines (the markings along a highway); in the dramatic use of the triangle; all this to a regularised emphatic beating sound on the soundtrack – *Peel* establishes the representation of a world dominated by attempts at ordering, a virtually mathematic image of life as calculation, constraint, control.

But in this early film-school effort by Campion, there is perhaps a third sense of the notion of discipline (one brought out all the more by the idea of an 'exercise'): that is, we can take the film itself to be a demonstration of the disciplined utilisation of established procedures of movie-making. Film-making itself is a craft involving training, expertise, understanding of physical laws (for example, the laws of optics), the application of practical rules, and some films, more clearly than others, signal their own status as

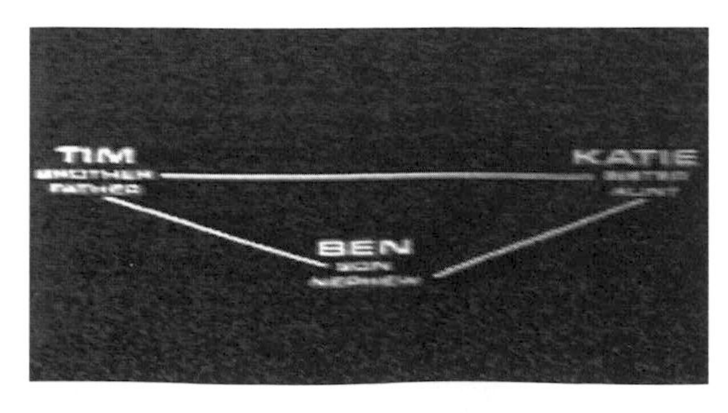

'The Geometry of discipline'

technical constructions rather than some sort of transparent reflections of the world filmed (think, for instance, of the films of Stanley Kubrick which take place in constructed and virtually science-fictional worlds where every aspect of the filming – from lighting to composition, to a mannered and even zombified acting style – reiterates how much his films are well-crafted, controlled objects). In this respect, *Peel* is very much a work that wants emphatically to show off its discipline, its confident mastery of the rules of cinema production. For the film-school students who made it, this is a film designed, it would seem, to recognise the disciplinarity of film school and thereby to vaunt an inescapably visible mastery of craft. At virtually every moment, a dramatically emphatic visual style signals the active effort of the film-makers to bring notice to their effort: extremely tight close-ups; framings in which the frame line intervenes to cut part of the image of people or things; shock cuts (for example, at one moment, we cut to a close-up of the sister's rear end as she squats to urinate); images designed around a dominant colour (the orange of the peel reiterated by the orange of the father and son's hair); visceral representations of intense tactility or palpability (for example, a tight close-up of a finger being inserted squishily among the sections of an orange). All of these effects announce an evident desire to use film style as a palpable subject of interest in its own right. (An anecdote: a friend of mine who teaches film and video-making told me he begins his introductory production classes with a showing of *Peel* [and also *Passionless Moments*]. As he recounted, the budding film-makers immediately understand the possibilities of film video as visual craft, as the creative application of learned procedures.)

Most of all, the film evidences a consistent and quite emphatic concern with a bold, striking compositional design. This design, which will remain as a constant and central aspect of many of the early films signed by Campion and often shot by Bongers, involves the placing of some objects or people in the extreme foreground of the shot (with the frame lines at the bottom or side of the image sometimes cutting them off) with other objects or persons placed in the extreme background. Take two shots from *Peel* in a sequence where the father has gone looking for his son who has run off after an attempt to discipline him. The first shot begins with the boy in extreme

'Playing with scale'

foreground alongside a road stretching into the background and ringed by trees. The boy is on the ground, scrunched over an orange whose peelings he has collected along the road and is trying to reconstitute. In the background the father approaches. Then, the son gets up and walks out of frame past the camera. We then cut to another shot, composed in great depth, in which the father is in the extreme foreground and the son is seen in extreme background (thus dramatically reversing the composition of the prior shot).

In moments such as these, a dramatic contrast is set up between the two spaces in the frame and is amplified often by additional elements. First, the placing of objects or persons at such distances from each other gives them contrasts of scale so that the close object or person appears enormous and the background object or person appears diminutive (this effect is further emphasised by a frequent use of wide-angle lenses which also amplify differences of scale from front to back and have the additional benefit for Campion's early surreality of appearing to bend, even to distort, foreground space in garish ways). Second, the objects or persons seem to have been deliberately posed into these compositions, thus again emphasising the appearance of artificiality (and this effect of a mannered, staged and even stagy composition is frequently amplified also by the editing which seems to jump in strikingly evident fashion from one garishly posed set-up to another). Interestingly, the sense of bold contrast between foreground can be further accentuated by converse strategies: on the one hand, there are shots that include little motion in the frame, thus directing the eye to study the composition (for example, a static shot of the sister in the back of the car with oranges on the dashboard looming up in the foreground); on the other hand, some shots have a character move from the far background to the foreground, or move from off-screen into the frame, making evident the plays of space and scale in the image (see colour section, between pp.90–1).

Yet another technique for amplifying the contrast of foreground and background has to do with colour contrasts in which the background and foreground have clashing dominant colours that are set off against each other. For example, in the shot of the sister in the back of the car, there is a visual play of contrasts between the luridly bright colour of the looming oranges in extreme foreground and the muted skin colour of the woman herself and the dark colour of her hair (significantly, she is the only member of the family not to have red hair and this enables her to have a particular visual effect in the film. (*After Hours*, as we will see later, takes the contrastive play of colours to its extreme.)

Peel flaunts a surreality of style that intersects in complicated ways with its subject matter. In particular, style takes off on its own, becoming something to be watched and luxuriated in for its own formal sake. This tension between an engagingly vivid style and a subject matter that is resonant because one can identity with it runs through the early film experiments of Campion. Indeed, if the fans of *The Piano* find in it a perfect match of style and story, we could even argue that that film's detractors frequently operate from a sense of a gap between story and style: Carol Clover's essay on the film argues, for instance, that the gorgeous style works to distract attention away from what for her is the masochistic sexual politics (Ada as suffering martyr) of the film's story.[10]

Passionless Moments (1983)

Passionless Moments was scripted by Gerard Lee (who is also listed as 'Ex-Director') and it appears that this was a film composed from a fair amount of collaboration around both subject matter and visual design. The film takes to an extreme a fascination, visible in other films signed by Campion, with the fragment, the seemingly pregnant instant, everyday life as a series of discrete events which flit around at the edge of meaning (see, for instance, the opening of *An Angel at My Table* which has flashes from Janet

Frame's early life that only later coalesce into the clear-cut narrative of a life). In *Passionless Moments*, bits drawn from the banalities of everyday experience appear as isolated and seemingly random anecdotes striving for significance. As the narrator intones at the film's end in a deep, authoritative voice (that can seem a parody of BBC omniscience), 'There are one million moments in your neighbourhood but, as the film-makers discovered, each has a fragile presence which fades almost as it forms.' Significantly, some filmographies list a longer title for the film, one that emphasises the modest anecdotal nature of the work: *Passionless Moments: Recorded in Sydney, Australia, Sunday October 2nd*.

In ten short sequences, each made up of a very few but generally strikingly composed shots, the film presents mini-narratives that hover between triviality and the suggestion of deeper import and importance. Each is introduced by a title and accompanied by a voice-over narration that explains the action transpiring and the thoughts of the people going through those actions: a man practising yoga creates new meanings from the slogan in a painting that he sees only bits of as he turns his head; a little boy plays at imagining that the groceries he is bringing home are a bomb that will explode unless he can get to his mother's kitchen in twenty seconds; a woman wonders about a noise coming from outside; two gay men are having problems in their relationship but one of them can only think about an issue of perception – why sight can't hold two things in focus at the same time; two neighbours who have been strangers wave to each other because of a misunderstanding; a man washing his jeans wonders about the meaning of a Monkees song that seems to him to be about jeans; a woman about to eat some ham is reminded of her uncle's pet pig (although this doesn't stop her from her meal); a man interrupts his ironing to remember how great he was in school sports and resolves to get back into shape; a man trying to put his life back together broods while lying on the floor of his home and looks up at the dust motes above him; a little girl who's sick at home becomes obsessed by the things that can fit onto a box of tissues and imagines grown-up men making this an issue of major research and discussion.

On the one hand, these anecdotes picture people stuck in the regularity of their existence. Thus, in the sketch about the ex-sports player (entitled

'Ed Played Front Row at School'), Ed is shown ironing and the narrator tells us that once a week Ed would iron the exact number of shirts in order to have his week planned out. This is a world of habit, of codified norms of social behaviours (for example, if you mistakenly believe that someone you don't know is waving at you, you wave back even if you don't know why). On the other hand, there are glimpses in some of the fragments of hopes, possibilities, dreams, that go beyond the given situation that people are sunk into. This is literally the case in the second episode, 'An Exciting One', where the little boy turns the banal task of bringing home his mother's shopping into a fictive high drama. Throughout, the mini-stories make manifest the efforts of imagination to transcend one's immediate situation and transport oneself elsewhere. In several of the stories, for instance, there is a dramatic cut from someone wondering or just thinking about something to that something as if cinema were directly visualising interior thought. For example, in the episode 'Angela Eats Meat', as the narrator tells us that the slice of ham reminds Angela of her uncle's pig, we cut from Angela about to put the ham into her mouth to a close-up of the pig. Likewise, when in the last sequence, Julie imagines authoritative men discussing the things that can fit on a tissue box, we are shown an image of those men at work. There is here a representation of the potentials of subjective imagining, and, in fact, several of the sequences offer first-person point-of-view shots as if to emphasise an origin of imaginative vision in individuals (for example, in the sequence of Gavin looking at the dust motes and remembering that 'his mother used to tell him they were angels', we are given a dreamy shot of the motes swirling around from Gavin's point of view).

But the film holds out little hope for the ability of imagination to sustain a transcendence of everyday reality. Thus, we see people who start by wondering about the mysteries of life but then retreat from a fascination with enigmas and fall back into the regularity of habit (for example, once 'Mrs Gwen Gilbert' discovers what the noise she's been hearing is [a neighbour beating laundry on a clothes line], she goes back to the activity she was engaged in – sorting flowers – before the puzzle arose). Furthermore, several of the sequences show the imagination of new possibilities as either ill-fated – not a real possibility for the future – or as coming from nostalgic memories of a past potential that the present can no longer offer. There is in the film a frequent sense of whimsical but also wistful regret at lost opportunities, lost chances to make something meaningful out of the course of life. (As we'll see later, regret over what might have been runs through many Campion films, culminating in the marital predicament of Isabel in *The Portrait of a Lady* and the missed chance at relationship for Ruth and P. J. in *Holy Smoke*). Take, for instance, the 'Ed Played Front Row At School' sequence. On the one hand, when Ed, standing at a window, suddenly remembers his schoolboy athleticism and jumps up energetically with a team cry, the film cuts to a sports team leaping up and crying as if responding to, as if manifesting, his imagination of a vitality of sports. Merging with Ed's own thoughts, the narrator talks of the glories of the past – 'What about that incredible pass?' – and announces that Ed's 'gonna give up the grog and get back into training'. On the other hand, this pronouncement (which in any case comes from Ed's own illusions rather than from the narrator's omniscient declaration of what will, in fact, happen) is belied by the image which shows Ed pouring himself a beer and then moving into the extreme foreground so that the bulge of his beer belly is emphasised.

Above all, the film adopts a comic tone towards its subjects, suggesting a silliness with their preoccupation to go beyond the given world by means of

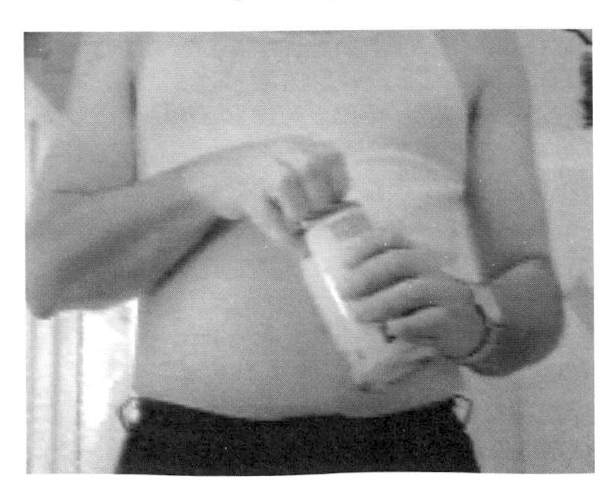

'Beer belly'

random acts of imagination and wonder. As banal as the people's lives might be, the mental transport that puzzling about enigmas and conceiving of alternate realities seem to offer is shown to be misguided in its own right. As Pam Cook puts it, 'gestures, games, body language and particularly verbal language are rife with often hilarious misunderstandings and double meanings'.[11] Thus, when in the episode 'Clear Up Sleepy Jeans', Jim wonders just what the lyrics to the Monkees song might mean – and we see an imagined image of a room filled with jeans that need to be sorted and arranged – there is the sense that this is a trivial use of imagination (and even a misguided one since the actual lyric is 'Cheer up, Sleepy Jean'). To be sure, the satire of the foibles of everyday life is also mixed with an affectionate recognition that we all engage in such trivial acts of imagination (thus, the narrator's last comments emphasise that such moments as we have seen exist 'in *your* neighbourhood') and participate in a general absurdity of everyday life. Thus, for instance, many of us have misheard or misinterpreted song lyrics and can more generally recognise our own errors in the characters of *Passionless Moments*.

The overall tone of the film is one of satire – of the characters, of us in our recognition that we do similar things. The satire is established first of all in the sheer silliness and even surreality of the human activities pictured: there is an incommensurability between the ordinariness of

'Clear up sleepy jeans'

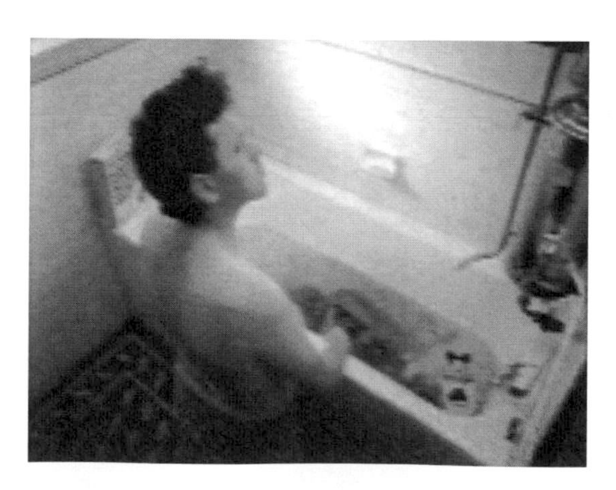

practices of daily life and the higher meanings we want to assign to them. In some cases, these higher meanings are shown to be constructed on the basis of epistemologically flimsy premises: a man who grants significance to the connection between random words he sees when he turns his head in one direction or another; a man who puzzles over incorrect lyrics of a song; neighbours who form a momentary bond and then realise their greeting to each other was based on misunderstanding. Additionally, filmic style intervenes to comment on human foibles and puncture their pretension. In particular, abrupt cuts from present reality to the content of acts of imagining work to set up contrasts between these two realms. For instance, the cuts to the school team both represent a power of Ed's imagination (by sheer will, he seems to call the team into existence) and a reminder of the concrete inescapability of present reality (Ed can only recapture past sports glory through nostalgic recollection; his body and daily habits will defeat his resolve to regain that past practically rather than just imaginatively). Likewise, in the episode in which 'Mrs Gwen Gilbert' wonders if the noise she is hearing outside could be a woodpecker, there is a cut to an animated cartoon of a woodpecker doing his stuff (not unlike the whimsical abrupt cut to the cartoon of Flora's father going up in flames in *The Piano*), a directly comical version of imagination. Moreover, when the narrator, speaking both for himself and Gwen, notes that 'we don't have woodpeckers in Australia', another cut to the cartoon reveals the bird stopping his pecking as if to remind us of the misguided nature of Gwen's initial supposition.

The surreality of everyday foibles in *Passionless Moments* comes not only from the nature of the situations themselves but from the stylistic treatment the film gives them. Like *Peel*, *Passionless Moments* is an exercise in the discipline of film-making that makes style itself visible, palpable. In particular, it uses extreme close-ups (with a concomitant cropping off of parts of objects filmed, such as bodies, through an overly tight framing that both includes and excludes); looks at the camera; noticeably abrupt cuts; a mixing of media (words, cartoons, as well as images of people and things); emphatic composition (for example, the first shot shows Ibrahim, the yoga practitioner, in the foreground, posed starkly with his fleshy body against the angular corners of his room); recurrent point-of-view shots that speak self-reflexively of the act of seeing. Most of all, striking effects of composition are emphasised and thereby rendered palpable through a recurrent technique (also central, as we've seen, in *Peel*) of setting up very sharp contrasts between objects looming up in the foreground and the rest of an environment glimpsed in the back of the frame. Contrast between close and distant space is also intensified by a frequent shooting from a low angle that brings characters ever more into the foreground and makes the space behind them seem like something bent away but also crushing in. In particular, several shots from the sequence of the gay couple, Shaun and Arnold, offer a self-reflexive representation of the contrast of spaces in ways that could be taken as a summary of the technique: we cut from a dramatically composed shot of Shaun in extreme foreground with Arnold as a smaller figure peeking up in the background (and with the contrast of background and foreground emphasised all the more by Shaun's movement of his thumb ever closer to the camera) to a subjective shot from Shaun's point of view in which his thumb and a studded dog collar in the background are caught up in modulating plays of focus and blur. This sequence, entitled 'Focal Lengths', renders literal the film's overall concern with variability of scale.

Some critics have seen a touch of David Lynch in Campion's films – and Campion herself acknowledges the influence: 'David Lynch and Jim Jarmusch, they're my modern film heroes.'[12] (Later in her career, she offers

'Focal lengths'

a direct homage by using noted Lynch music composer Angelo Badalamenti to score the music for *Holy Smoke.*) Certainly, some of the early films such as *Passionless Moments* come close to approximating the feel of Lynch films. There is in both film-makers, for instance, a concern with common ways of life that are rendered comic in their triviality and in the incommensurability between situation and imagination; a depiction of the ways ordinary existence harbours potentials for weirdness; likewise, a suspicion that human contact, even of the most seemingly banal sort, harbours tensions, conflicts, alienation; an extreme and often highly visceral emphasis on the tactile, on a world rendered massively palpable; a fascination with a transcendence that is often deflated and revealed to be a fiction; a breakdown of narrative into little bits in which people parade their foibles before the camera; an arrangement of characters in highly staged and highly artificial poses that make them veritable puppets manipulated by a cinematic *mise-en-scène*; a fragmentation, through cutting and framing, of the body into isolated parts fetishised by the close view of the camera.

A Girl's Own Story (1984)

A Girl's Own Story shares many of the demonstrative, highly marked traits of bold style evident in *Peel* and *Passionless Moments*, but, as critical response to it especially by feminists indicates, it can have an emotional bite, a psychological resonance, that distinguishes it from the other early works. Some of the intensity of the film comes from the fact, no doubt, that stylistic procedures that in the earlier films were designed to create strangeness and a weird humour are now being employed in service of a tale about recognisable entrapments and dilemmas of a particularly intense and consequential sort. This is a film whose story deals with real-life crises that young adolescent girls can confront – sexual confusion, family strife, incest (a girl made pregnant by her brother), molestation (the young heroine dragged into a car by a mysterious man). Not for nothing has one feminist commentator inscribed the film within a tradition of representations of problems in the construction of girls' identity.[13]

To be sure, *Peel* had dealt with the everyday problems of a group of family members and one could certainly imagine that their situation might

Real life crises

actually exist (indeed, the three figures in *Peel* are played by the actual family members who were evidently living through the very sorts of familial tensions and antagonisms depicted in the film). But the extreme nature of *Peel*'s garish techniques (for example, the intense contrast between big images in the foreground and tiny ones in the background) is coupled with a depiction of the family members as tacky in a way that makes this narrative universe seem distant from ours. With their loud, trashy clothes, these people are constituted as an object of satire for the audience to feel superior to. (As we will see, many of the Campion films take up an attitude of superiority to a way of life deemed to be low in its crassness, crudity and kitschiness. *Peel* already announces this concern to mock the lifestyles of low-brow culture.) *Passionless Moments* also deals with everyday life but there too a comic distance and even superiority is created. In fact, the film sets out to depict a certain absurdity to daily life by measuring the breach between the ways ordinary people try to create mystery, excitement, hope and dreams, and the very meagre, banal materials that they are basing their acts of imagination upon. The distance between reality and imagination then feeds into a distance the viewer can take towards the characters and their trivialising foibles.

In contrast, while *A Girl's Own Story* does have some images of kitschy and comic behaviour – for example, a shot of three girls singing Beatles songs with the three of them arrayed in a composition that contrasts one in

Remnants of quirky composition

the extreme foreground to the other two in the far background – the corniness of the behaviour here is not equated with a whole lifestyle but with momentary performances by people who are testing modes of being against the vagaries of the world. Quirkiness becomes narrativised as the strangeness that one inevitably encounters in growing up and negotiating the world. In particular, the girls in *A Girl's Own Story* are shown to be caught up in a moment of transition between childhood, adolescence and young adulthood, and are trying out various identities and often fumbling as they do so. The potential strangeness of some of the ways they attempt to do this – for example, when two of the girls try to imagine what it would be like to be kissed by a Beatle, one puts on a Beatles mask and the two begin to make out – is rendered touching and even in some cases is a source of sadness and nostalgia.

It is perhaps notable that where the title of *Peel* refers impersonally to an object and *Passionless Moments* signals a critical attitude toward an aggregate of human activities, the title of *A Girl's Own Story* personalises the narrative, makes it the possession of a specific figure. Just as adolescents often keep diaries that recount the transitions in their life, the film has a testimonial quality to it, and this leads it to move closer to its central character, to foster a greater degree of identification. Indeed, *A Girl's Own Story* exhibits, from its opening scene of girls looking at a drawing of male genitalia in a book, a much greater and quite systematic employment of point-of-view shots than the other shorts, making sights pass through the characters (and, by proxy, through the spectator). Indeed, the drawing sports a caption that indicates 'This sight may shock young girls' and the film is indeed in many ways about the risks such girls are open to as they proceed through the messy business of growing into young women. For all its strangeness, this is a film that chronicles very real issues of girls' survival in a modern, menacing world.

Peel and *Passionless Moments* both create painful comedy from the over-investment people make in ultimately trivial coincidence: in the former, a few meagre orange peels become the occasion for the meltdown of a family; in the latter, ordinary persons flirt with a universe of the seemingly extraordinary which is ultimately inaccessible to them. (An Australian film scholar has suggested to me that the oranges in *Peel* may be an in-joke reference to director Gillian Armstrong for whom oranges are a recurrent image.) In contrast, *A Girl's Own Story* fosters the spectator's closeness to its primary characters and suggests that small and seemingly trivial details of everyday existence can be quite consequential for the way one lives one's life. For the cold geometric rigour of the lettering and diagram that opens *Peel*, *A Girl's Own Story* substitutes a title in flowery script, already signalling a move into a more personalised, even sentimentalised register. A number of qualities encourage a greater emotional, involved spectatorial response to this film: for example, the point-of-view editing that I've already mentioned; an acting style that hints at psychological complexity (unlike, say, *Peel* where characters often become veritable automatons under the pressure of family relation); a romantic use of music to signal affect (for example, the lachrymose tune 'Somewhere My Love' plays over several scenes); a sensuousness of objects heightened through an emphasis on tactility (for example, in the opening scene, a girl's fingers trace over the drawing of genitalia); a concomitant emphasis on the physical immediacy of the act of kissing (as in an early scene where two girls wander around Pam's bedroom and kiss the Beatles pictures she has posted up everywhere).

Consequently, when the end of the film offers up the bizarre spectacle of Pam, the protagonist, singing 'I feel the cold' while images of ice-skating are projected onto her body and she seems to float against an inky void,

'I feel the cold'

what appears to be a homage to David Lynch (the disconnected, floating figures of *Eraserhead*) can also seem more psychologically and emotionally resonant than Lynch's surreal, distanced strangeness. Pam has been through a lot (including perhaps being molested when younger), and the song serves as an expression of her situation of solitude, vulnerability and despair. Indeed, if the song becomes an embodiment of the agonies Pam has been living through, such externalisation of inner turmoil seems appropriate since so much of the film is about the ways the psychology of emotion becomes corporealised in the ways people act and appear. *A Girl's Own Story* is in large part an expressionist work in which visual style is not so much imposed on characters from a narrational distance as seeming to arise as a direct correlate of characters' inner emotions. Young women here are as they are because they have responded both mentally and bodily to the traumas that beset them and that they reflect and rework in their very behaviour.

As Freda Freiberg suggests in one of the earliest essays on Jane Campion's cinema, the lyrics of Pam's songs are quite apt since, as Freiberg puts it, 'In a world without tenderness, and full of sexual fears, the girls "feel the cold."'[14] Indeed, Freiberg goes on to note how this final reference to cold is, in fact, the conclusion of a motif that runs through the whole film of the tension between a desired warmth and the coldness that the girls too often end up with: from an early scene of two girls staring at radiators as they prepare to mime kissing and being kissed by a Beatle to the pregnant girl, Gloria, alone and isolated in the cold of a home for unmarried mothers, the film depicts adolescent life as mere pockets of furtive warmth surrounded by inky pools of chilliness. In Freiberg's words,

> Their desires [i.e. those of these girls], especially their craving for warmth are linked to two particular images – radiators and kittens – which recur throughout the film. The kittens appear to represent the girls' desire for warmth and love, but also, like Colette's cats, they seem to symbolise female sexuality. … The girls are associated together in a common plight, even though Gloria alone suffers the stigma of unmarried motherhood, through their common experience of 'the cold' and their similar appearance (they are all gawky adolescent girls, brunette, bespectacled, dressed in winter school tunics or dressing gowns and slippers).[15]

A Girl's Own Story depicts a number of incidents in a young woman's life that can harbour intense emotional resonance: the common experience of rejection by one's peers, the complications of sexual maturation, and even literally a malevolent side of sexuality (this, after all, is a film about, among other things, incest and child molestation). The moments of *A Girl's Own Story* are far from passionless – although it is a passion of an often dangerous and consequent sort – and the film concentrates on how the protagonists experience, feel, the moments of their life.

After Hours (1984)

Offered up in fragments that are often not in chronological order, *After Hours* deals with an investigation of sexual harassment in the workplace. But it too exhibits tensions of style and subject that sometimes make it difficult to decide univocally the politics of the film. For example, for all its emphasis on sexual threat, it is like *A Girl's Own Story* which functions in large part also as a formal exercise in which in its case abuse, molestation and incest can turn into further examples of weirdness rather than a relevant social-sexual problem. From the first scene in which the victim, Lorraine (Danielle Pearse), whose hobby is swimming, is questioned by an official investigator (Anna-Maria Monticelli), a series of flashbacks show

how Lorraine's boss, Mr Phillips (Don Reid), tried to seduce her when he had virtually blackmailed her into staying late at the office (by threatening to harp on her lateness to work from her morning swimming practice). The chronicle of the harassment is intercut in temporally ambiguous ways with the investigation and with scenes of people in Lorraine's life who fail to offer her full support through the aftermath of her traumatic experience: her boyfriend, her mother, co-workers, Mr Phillips's secretary and Lorraine's coach. By the end of this twenty-five minute film, when errors appear in Lorraine's recollection, even the initially sympathetic investigator seems to have lost faith in the strength of Lorraine's case – perhaps even its veracity – and she sets out to dissuade Lorraine from taking the case to court. We learn also that Lorraine has lost her job.

Everyone and everything – including her own memory – work against Lorraine, making her situation unwinnable. Against the film's institutional status as a work of feminist activism (made by a women's collective to militate around issues of harassment), it would be easy to read the film's pessimism as leading to a quietism: so many things will conspire against a young woman victimised by harassment that it is not worth her trying to fight. As Lorraine herself declares to her mother, 'I'd rather forget the whole thing', and by the end of the film, she appears to have lapsed into a dulled resignation and passivity. (Ironically, in interviews, Jane Campion also declares that she would like to forget the experience of making this film.)

After Hours is far from being a film of evident commitment, community and feminist solidarity. Even Lorraine's own mother offers no real support and instead can only criticise her daughter for having worn a miniskirt, which she implies is provocative, to work. The conversation between Lorraine and her mother is highly conflictual (and there are hints of other tensions in the family when the mother begins to fight with her other daughter), and in a later scene when Lorraine, caught up in her thoughts about the incident, is spinning a backyard clothes-drying rack around and around, her mother can do nothing else than exhibit strong impatience with her daughter. Similarly, Mr Phillips's elderly secretary comes into his office after the harassment incident to declare her support of him, thus showing us a woman in support of a suspect man. In fact, as the secretary's expression of faith in her boss suggests, if there is any solidarity in this world of power relations, it is between some women and the powerful men they are in thrall to (as we saw in the discussion of *The Piano*, women's dependency on men, even in potentially masochistic situations, may be central to Campion's cinema). One very telling scene has Phillips go to ask advice about his harassment suit from a fellow businessman he meets at a bar/dance hall. The businessman is accompanied by a young woman whom he introduces as his 'secretary' but an extreme close-up shows her putting her hand on his thigh, making it clear that she is his mistress. She dotes on her boss's every word and command and shows no interest in Lorraine's case other than to wonder if Lorraine is broad-shouldered from her swimming practice. Interestingly, when Phillips and the woman are first presented to each other, he declares that he knows her already and she nervously denies that. There is the suggestion, but it is not made explicit, that perhaps there has been something sexual between the two of them (a close-up of Phillips noticing the hand on the thigh indicates his unease), a hint again at the ties of women to more powerful men. Additionally, when the boss asks the woman to leave the men alone for a moment so they can talk man-to-man, she readily and devotedly absents herself, cooing and kissing at the boss and going off to dance in the background. The image here is of woman as obedient in her subordination to a man and having no will of her own. Revealingly, as she dances, the boss leers at her and asks Phillips if he would like to dance with her (Phillips declines). There is a hint here of the ways in which men casually engage in what feminist anthropologists call a 'traffic in women', in which women are treated as commodities to be traded in order to solidify male bonding.

There is very clearly in *After Hours* the representation of a world in which women have bought into relations of power and into a system that defines success in terms of material acquisition. Typical in this respect is the depiction of Phillips's wife who, in her two scenes, is shown to have no interests other than landscaping, decoration and interior design. She is totally a slave of the prettified look of things. Thus, when her husband explains to her the operation of massive water tanks (is this the realm he works in?), she can only respond to his technical explanations by declaring that the industrial site could use a woman's touch with flowers planted to prettify things. Likewise, when her husband broods over the charges of harassment brought against him, the wife is shown as so caught up in her decorating plans for their suburban house that she is clueless about her husband's worries and offers him no solace. The wife is a figure who trivialises things in her obsession with a superficial look attainable through mere decoration.

Women in *After Hours* do not stand up for other women. For example, in a way that anticipates Kay's work world in *Sweetie*, Lorraine's co-workers are seen to have an active antagonism to her for no apparent reason other than some sort of automatic and natural cattiness and rivalry. For example, when she comes in late to the office and asks if one of the other members of staff couldn't have taken off the cover of her typewriter for her, one coldly replies that, no, they couldn't. Likewise, another worker seems to take pleasure in announcing that Mr Phillips wishes to see Lorraine (presumably because she was late arriving at the office) and clearly relishes the idea of Lorraine's chastisement or even punishment. Later on, when Lorraine has been fired, the co-workers immediately battle for possession of her typewriter, like vultures profiting from her misfortune. (For what it's worth, there seems to be no love lost among these other co-workers either, and it appears in the film that the women automatically and naturally adopt a cattiness towards their fellow workers in general. For example, when a disabled co-worker asks if anyone can get her a cup of coffee, all the women, except Lorraine, refuse to help.) To be sure, there is a vague hint of empathy between Lorraine and one co-worker, the disabled woman, but the connection of the two women is so minor as to offer no real sense of unity. Additionally, the handicapped woman has a meeting with the investigator in which her own cynicism about anything being done to remedy the situation of harassment and her reticence to help are quite evident.

That we see this relatively insignificant character in a private conversation with the investigator about Lorraine, a conversation that could certainly have consequences for how Lorraine's story is to be regarded and treated, is in keeping with a motif that runs through a number of Campion films. Specifically, whatever the personal agency that people – women, especially –

are supposed to have in their everyday lives, its advance is frequently shown to be limited by conversations and machinations that concern them but that they are not privy to. People talk and plot about others. Obviously, the extreme example is *The Portrait of a Lady* where Gilbert Osmond and Madame Merle conspire to plot Isabel's future (but where Ralph Touchett and his father also negotiate between themselves about her fate). But the image of the individual as object of discussions that can easily constitute schemes of control is omnipresent: Sweetie's family planning the trick that will leave her behind when they go on a trip; Janet Frame's professor (on whom she has a crush) arranging with officials to have her committed; Ada's father forcing her to marry a man she's 'not yet met', and Baines and Stewart negotiating over piano lessons on Ada's piano; Ruth's family in *Holy Smoke* arranging without her knowledge to have her incarcerated with an 'exit counsellor' to have her de-programmed from her cult. Likewise, Lorraine in *After Hours* is someone others observe with intent curiosity and they converse about and scheme about in consequential ways.

If *After Hours* seems to contradict an activist intent through its pessimism and its depiction of a conflictual world with little sense of community in it, the style of the film frequently also diverges from direct concern with its ostensible subject matter (sexual harassment) to set up engrossing visual games that become subjects of interest in their own right. Take, for instance, a series of shots that follow the opening scene of discussion between Lorraine and the investigator. From a fairly conventional rendition of a dialogue scene, the film offers a shock cut to an image from below of swimmers in a pool followed by an insistent tracking shot laterally across the frame in which we see swimmers lounging alongside the pool and arranged so that they take up planes from the extreme foreground to the back (that contrastive play of spaces that we saw in the early shorts). There is then a two-shot mini-sequence in which Lorraine speaks to her coach and then he responds; in both shots, the person speaking is shown in extreme close-up and a bit off to the side of the frame, creating a weird and boldly emphatic composition (with some distortion of these faces that are so close to the camera lens). This is followed by a shot of Lorraine coming into the frame, in which she first appears as a torso with the rest of her body cut off by the frame lines. Lorraine readies herself for swimming and looks down at the water. The next shot offers a high-angle view of the pool, and the logic of editing at first leads one to assume this is the reverse-shot of the previous one (in other words, water seen by Lorraine). But then we see Lorraine swim into this shot that we had previously imagined was from her point of view. There is then another shock cut to a close-up of Lorraine waving her hair back and forth to dry it. By a cut, we discover that Lorraine is now in her office as, looming up in the foreground, one of her co-workers addresses her while we see another worker small in the back of the frame. This is followed by a curious image of packages of chickens each with a woman's name on it in a refrigerator (later, we learn that the women store their food shopping for home in the office fridge, but it is left as a strange detail that we never resolve why these women would all have bought chicken specifically).

In addition to these complicated patterns of editing and of bold composition, the shots I have enumerated are also distinguished by bright pop-art colours and contrasts between them. For example, the blue of the pool water and of bathing suits and goggles is contrasted with the bright red of swim caps and of scarlet lipstick; in fact, in the very striking shot of Lorraine addressing her coach, the colours of lipstick, cap and goggles (not to mention a striking quality of skin colour through make-up and lighting, something that is also important in Ada's representation in *The Piano*) combine with elements of the composition (in the background, there is another swimmer also with brightly contrasting cap and goggles, the back of the frame thus mimicking the foreground in ways that anticipate *The Piano* where characters are frequently doubled by others in eerie fashion). Like *Sweetie*, *The Portrait of a Lady* and, in particular, *The Piano*, *After Hours* is visually a very designed film with many scenes emphasising either one intense colour (for example, the after-hours scenes in the office building are bathed in a creepy, somewhat fluorescent blueness not unlike the garish blue that dominates the look of so many shots in *The Piano*) or an intense clash of colours (the bright green walls of the investigator's office against which Lorraine's blue sweater stands out intensely).

The shots I've examined from *After Hours* do not coalesce into a simple and unified narrative structure. The shock cutting and the resultant initiation of new actions and new locales seemingly from within the heart of previous ones, the selective focusing on body parts, the violation of editing expectations (for example, the cut to Lorraine swimming that violates the convention that a cut after a shot of someone looking reveals the thing they were looking at), the emphatic, tight use of close-ups, all work to turn the unfolding of narrative into something resembling more a succession of fragments, everyday life as a disjunctive and even incoherent flow of bits (like the anecdotes that make up daily experience in *Passionless Moments*).

Visually, then, *After Hours* has many of the stylistic traits that are distinctive in Campion's early films: a composition that is rendered striking – and thereby exceeds mere communication of narrative – through sharp plays of discrete colours and through insistent framings that boldly contrast foreground and background; connected to that, a recurrent compositional style that in conversations between people puts one in the extreme foreground with the frame line dramatically cutting off half of the face; a disjunctive editing that makes narrative come to us in glimpses as unassimilated bits and pieces (like the opening of, say, *An Angel at My Table*); camera movements that do no storytelling and seem to exist for lyrical effect or to call attention to themselves; a poetic immersion in the elements (the water of the pool with bodies floating in it like Ada hovering above her piano); a visceral tactility (the flesh of bodies, the intensity of faces seen in close-up); a garish emphasis on bizarre imagery (the chickens in the fridge, with the last shot of the film devoted to a long take in which Phillips's secretary wanders around the office trying to decide what to do now that Lorraine has been fired and the chicken has gone bad); a blocking of characters in quite artificially arranged poses that virtually turn them into figures manipulated by a staging (a compositional strategy self-reflexively commented on in one shot where Phillips himself in the extreme foreground composes his wife in the background against the backdrop of the water tanks); a rendering strange of originally ordinary locales (thus, when Lorraine's boyfriend confronts her and implies that she didn't do enough to stop the harassment, the scene takes place in the bottom of a drained pool with the two characters posed dramatically between foreground and background; moreover, the shot continues the stark contrast of colours through blue strips on the pool's bottom, a red cover posed in the background and a bright red book in the foreground under the boyfriend's arm).

Campion herself implies in interviews that *After Hours* holds style in check to enable the unambiguous, didactic presentation of a political theme. I should note, indeed, that Campion chooses to distance herself from the film, going so far as to virtually disavow authorship of it. Yet as close analysis reveals, *After Hours* is a film of evident stylistic play and experimentation with some of the images exhibiting a degree of lyricism. Just as we find in *The Piano* a poetic fascination with water, *After Hours* is a film that offers poetic images of the aquatic realm: two scenes of swimmers shot from below in the pool; the curious shot that we mistakenly assume is from Lorraine's point of view and in which we see light play across the surface of the pool as she swims into view; a long shot from above of swimmers performing splashy turns in the water. Most striking is a last sequence of Lorraine at the pool. Preceded by a sequence in which the unpunished Phillips plays with his German shepherd and followed by the surreal and bizarre end-of-film shot of the secretary scurrying around the office with the rotting chicken, this sequence begins with a shock cut to a hand (revealed to be Lorraine's) playing over a shimmering surface of water that it caresses every so lightly creating concentric flutterings. Lorraine appears to just fall over into the water – there are several shots of her from underneath first sinking to the bottom and then floating passively. This is the last time we see Lorraine. Her social world has failed her and all that is left for her is poetic immersion in that space where, as the end of *The Piano* tells us, 'there is a silence where no sound may be'.

At the same time, for all the way in which stylistic play can become the actual point of interest of the film, it is necessary to note that there is one way in which these striking stylistics are often in concert with one particular content, one that recurs in several Campion films. Specifically, the garishness of imagery is frequently associated with a garishness of certain classes of people. From the satires of suburbia in *Sweetie* and *Holy Smoke* to the distinction of Ada from the Maori people and from old biddies like Aunt Morag and Nessie to the representation of masculine inadequacy in men like Stewart or Janet Frame's awkward and unendearing neighbour in London to Ruth's mother in *Holy Smoke*, unable to throw off her suburban prejudices and be open to the Indian experience, there appears to be evident in Campion's work a degree of cultural elitism which imagines that there is a hierarchy of distinction in which some people have more or less refinement and value than others (and those lacking in distinction are to be mocked). As we noted already with regards to *Peel* and *Passionless Moments*, Campion protagonists frequently have to fight for independence in a crass world of tasteless vulgarians (just as her films themselves – as works of art cinema – have to mark their distinction from the supposed cultural inadequacies of more mainstream, commercial film). That *After Hours* associates this representation of tacky kitsch culture with women primarily – the wife who can only prattle on about her design and landscape ideas; the co-workers who are overly made-up, who in so many ways lack Lorraine's prettiness, and who seem to incarnate a cultural cheesiness (with one scene even beginning with an extreme close-up of one worker applying her bright lipstick) – suggests that the film is no easy work of feminine solidarity (between characters, but also between the director/scriptwriter and those characters). There are, perhaps, class limits to Campion's representation of sexuality and community, just as some critics of *The Piano* argue that Ada's eroticism is contrasted to, and thus valorised by, the earthy unrefinement of the Maori people. *After Hours* may itself criticise male-imposed norms of feminine beauty – the disabled woman explains to the investigator that Phillips could not be interested in a woman like her – but it also participates in a hierarchising around such norms and legitimates a charged version of taste and social/cultural distinction.

The Early Features

Two Friends (1986)

In 1986, producer Jan Chapman approached Campion to do a television feature for the Australian Broadcasting Co. and through this there began a collaboration/friendship between the two women that would culminate in

The Piano, which Chapman also produced. The telefilm was *Two Friends* and was scripted by author Helen Garner, known as a writer of social realist drama (later, she would also write the screenplay for Gillian Armstrong's *The Last Days of Chez Nous* [1992] and the two screenplays have been published together).[16] Significantly, while some critics have tried to suggest that the film's complicated narrative structure is in keeping with a Campion concern to find innovative ways to tell stories – the telefilm begins with the two teenage friends, Louise and Kelly, having broken up, and then proceeds through a series of flashbacks that move in reverse chronological order to ever earlier moments – the shape of the narrative comes, in fact, from Garner and is something that Campion didn't find to her own taste: as she puts it, 'I also liked the script a lot even if the idea of telling a story by going back in time was not what I would have chosen.'[17] Additionally, Campion had to make do with a technical crew not of her own choosing, although she does seem to have had some creative input into the look of the film: as she says,

> I like to look in the viewfinder because I am very precise about the frame that I want. During the shooting of *Two Friends*, the crew under the director of photography felt some resentment towards me because they weren't used to a director who deals with things like that. My director of photography didn't understand what I wanted very well and I had to be very obstinate to impose my views. ... I had to use the television crew. They were very competent, but we simply had different methods of shooting.[18]

Beyond its striking reverse-chronology narrative structure, *Two Friends* has a number of other distinctive stylistic traits. First of all, the complication of narrative logic derives not only from the play with chronology, but with a concomitant ambiguity that derives from the fact that, even in order, narrative developments frequently come only as understated bits: for instance, only by watching very closely does one come to realise that Louise's mother and father have split up since this is never directly made an issue in any of the narrative moments. Moreover, in both its reverse-chronological presentation and the correct chronology of the original story, *Two Friends* operates through an *in media res* structuring that leaves causes and effects of individual narrative developments unexplained even if one can sort out their place in the overall temporal order. For instance, the first segment of the film begins abruptly with Louise's parents arriving for the funeral of a young girl – a situation that is presented as an isolated anecdote without prior explanation and serving primarily to set the tone of a story that will be about the complications for adolescents in growing up into young adulthood. Additionally, the segment ends with Louise receiving a reconciliatory letter from Kelly and reflecting upon it: there is no indication of just what Louise will do, and as the rest of the film moves progressively into the past, it becomes ever more apparent that the chronological endpoint of the narrative is Louise's indecision over Kelly's letter.

The fragmentation of the narrative into virtually anecdotal bits that only add up vaguely to a coherent and cohesive story is amplified by a distinctive style at the level of the framing, composing and shooting of individual shots. First of all, segments tend to be made up of a few long takes (with little or no camera movement) in which major developments are played out in the space and time of a unitary scene. Perhaps most striking in this respect is a long single-shot sequence in which Kelly's father leaves her alone with one of his mates when he goes out to meet a girlfriend: for over two minutes, the shot chronicles the dad's departure, Kelly and the mate watching TV until boredom overtakes them, their decision to play a board game and Kelly's exhortation to him to get more comfortable, all of this overladen with a tone of potential risk for this young woman alone with an older man (a risk that will materialise in the next scene when the man tries to seduce Kelly). The way such scenes play themselves out within the length of a single shot tends to give them an independence from each other that reiterates their uniqueness and their anecdotalism. At the same time, the long take participates in thattension between style and subject that I've been suggesting is part of the art-cinema experimentalism of the early works: the long take allows resonant psycho-social situations to play themselves out (for example, an adolescent girl vulnerable to the sexual power and exploitation of a much older man), but it also becomes one more piece in a stylistic game that focuses attention on its own formal permutations, such as the ways characters move through space in choreographed fashion.

For instance, the long takes are frequently filled with the coming and going of characters in and out of the frame, reminding the viewer of off-screen space but making it into a veritable void that surrounds the on-screen action and clearly demarcates it. Take, for instance, an early scene in which Louise comes home to find her boyfriend, Matthew, waiting for her: the shot begins with him alone in the frame, pacing with impatience; then, Louise comes into frame, greets him and moves off-screen only to return an instant later; next, Louise's mother crosses the on-screen space as she goes to the kitchen to make tea; Louise and Matthew talk for a while about Kelly and the fact that she's living a sort of punkish existence at the margins of society; Louise goes off-screen and back, once again; the conversation continues, then we cut to a brief high shot of Louise's mother alone in the kitchen. Via a second cut we return to the set-up of the long take and the off-screen/on-screen dialectic continues as the mother comes back into frame, stands in front of Louise and blocks our view of her, then exits off-screen once again. The shot finally ends when the boyfriend also exits the frame to put on a record. In a film that is so much about the tentativeness of relationships – between best friends, boy and girl, husband and wife, parents and children, siblings – the blocking here offers a literal embodiment of human interaction as an interweaving of connection and disconnection, contact and separation. It is appropriate that the cutaway that interrupts this long take is to the mother by herself in the kitchen, for one subplot of the film has to do with her increasing sense of being excluded from her daughter's life and the world of youth (an exclusion also dramatically represented in a later scene when Kelly, Louise and the mother are returning by metro from a shopping outing and the two girls choose to sit by themselves, apart from the older woman).

Two Friends' systematic employment of boldly composed long shots breaks narrative flow into a series of self-sufficient tableaux. There are few match-cuts to adjoining spaces in the film, and there are few shot/reverse-shots that would establish clearly the spatial relation of one character to another. For instance, in the above-described sequence of Louise and her boyfriend, when there is the cutaway to the mother alone in her kitchen, we can make a vague guess as to where this space is, but its exact spatial relationship to the scene of Louise and her boyfriend is unclear and only reiterates the mother's sense of being cut off from her daughter's adolescent universe.

As the contact and disconnection in the scene of Louise, her mother and her boyfriend all moving in and out of frame in the space of the home suggests, *Two Friends* sometimes uses its boldness of imagery in service of the story. That is, the film tries to offer narrative motivations and thematic justification for its strangeness of look, making disjunctions serve as a figure for the fragility of human interconnections. The film doesn't exclusively show off style for the sake of style (with the exception, perhaps, of a long sequence towards the end of the film in which parts of the image are animated or scratched over), but frequently narrates a resonant story that viewers can identify with emotionally. Indeed, for all the emphatic and mannered look of its shots, *Two Friends* is like *A Girl's Own Story* in using a strange style to hint at dangers, tensions, a fraughtness of emotion in everyday situations – especially those faced by young adolescent women – more than to suggest simply a comically weird surreality. As its title implies, this is a film about a relationship – how it begins, how it develops, how it can fall apart – and it even goes beyond the concentration on just Louise and Kelly to offer a depiction of a wide range of ways people come together and separate (for example, husbands and wives, parents and children). Moreover, the formation and/or maintenance of most of the two-person relationships in the film comes at a cost of the cutting off, or taking for granted, of a third party. Thus, in one scene, Louise introduces Kelly and her boyfriend, and a series of shots depict his increasing separation from the two girls. For instance, in one long shot that lasts over a minute, the two girls look gleefully at a scrapbook while the bored Matthew sulks, paces the room, picks up a magazine and comes to sit down in the extreme foreground, the frame line cutting him off and revealing only his knees and hands. At the same time, there is no positing here of Kelly and Louise's relationship as any more durable (in fact, the reverse-order chronology reveals that at the story's end, Louise has opted for Matthew and broken with Kelly) and the shot ends with Louise leaving the on-screen space, hurt and embarrassed, when Kelly tells Matthew that Louise wears a dental plate.

The narrative universe of *Two Friends* is one in which people try to reach out to each other and fumble as they do so, forming alliances that are vulnerable at best and awkward – even conflictual or dangerous – at worst. For instance, while the two young women, Louise and Kelly, are trying to negotiate a world of sexuality and even reaching out willingly to it (like the girls in *A Girl's Own Story* who start the film by looking curiously at the image of male genitalia), the film suggests that sexuality is something that can be made malevolent in cases where older figures take advantage of the young (as in the scene of Kelly receiving sexual advances from her father's friend).

Even the seemingly privileged relationship between women reveals its fragility. Significantly, while from its title on the film does imply a special and privileged connection between the girls, woman-to-woman relations are revealed to be as fraught as any other. On the one hand, women have a unique bond. For instance, isolated as she is from her daughter's world, Louise's mother is shown to be able to take solace in the friendship of a woman her own age (in one scene, when the girls are having a teenage rock party at Louise's house, the two mothers hide out upstairs and comment on the sexual fumblings of the children). And other women also seem to have unique forms of connection. Thus, in a scene that anticipates the mimicry between Ada and Flora in *The Piano*, Kelly watches television on the floor with her little sister who begins to ape every gesture of her older sibling. Yet, the intensity of these bonds can cause conflict. After all, despite its title, the film begins with Louise and Kelly already out of sorts with each other. The opening sequence is one in which Louise and Kelly do not meet.

Significantly, the end of this first segment (which is chronologically the last development in the film and which has Louise receiving the letter of reconciliation from Kelly) immediately indicates a lack of connection between the two young women. On the one hand, a voice-over from Kelly narrates the contents of her letter (she has a new boyfriend, she lost her cat, etc.). On the other hand, as the voice-over continues, Louise leaves the table she's been reading at and moves, via a cut, to her piano where she plays loudly, the sound of her practice conflicting directly with the audibility of Kelly's message. Louise retreats into her piano-playing in opposition to Kelly's attempts at re-bonding. In fact, a motif of sound – such as the piano lesson that Louise uses to try to escape into her own personal space – as something that separates as much as it unites people runs through the film. Take, for instance, two successive shots: first, Louise is out driving with her mother and shushes her attempts to start up a conversation to listen instead to what's on the radio; then, we see the mother alone in a room of their house, brooding as Kelly practises her French horn somewhere off-screen.

In the early scene of Louise at the piano, it is not clear whether she has actually read the letter through, and there's a curious sense of conflict as Louise begins to pound the piano keys all the more stridently as Kelly's voice-over continues. It's as if in some way the tensions she feels about Kelly continue to resonate in her head. There is a direct representation here of two worlds at odds with each other. The film affirms girls' friendship, but it also suggests that there is an inevitability that in growing up, girls may develop new priorities that leave old friendships behind. Just as Louise's mother increasingly appears to be left out of her daughter's world, so too do Kelly and Louise move into different orbits in which their interests no longer coincide. *Two Friends* is ultimately a sad film full of regret for the friendships that were and can never be again.

Sweetie (1989)

The stylistic features that enable the early shorts to distance themselves from the real-world coordinates in their subject matter are on full display in *Sweetie* and make this feature a work of intense visual and narrative strangeness. We can sum up the film's overall deviations in style by suggesting that they take place at two levels. On the one hand, as we've seen with the Campion shorts, the transition from shot to shot or scene to scene is often handled through abrupt cuts that contrast strikingly divergent compositions and, frequently, clashes of colour or scale. On the other hand, within individual shots, Sally Bongers's cinematography renders reality unreal, even grotesque. Feminist theorist Anneke Smelik offers an apt and

Longing (*The Piano*, 1993) (see p.26)

Longing (*The Piano*, 1993) (see p.28)

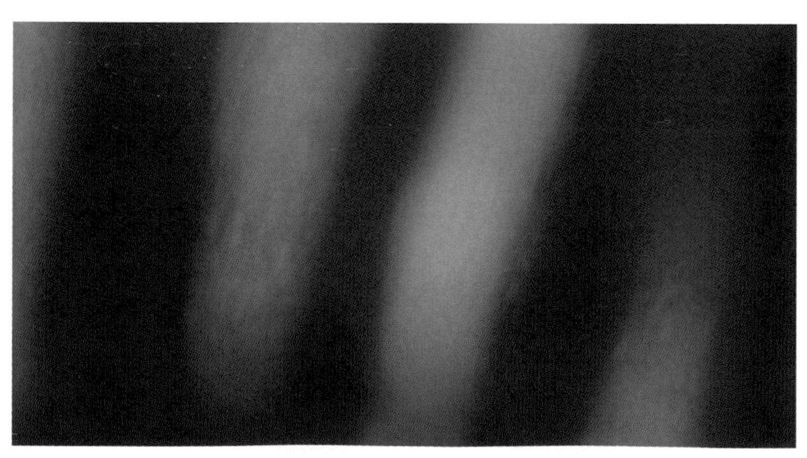

The first shot (*The Piano*, 1993) (see p.32)

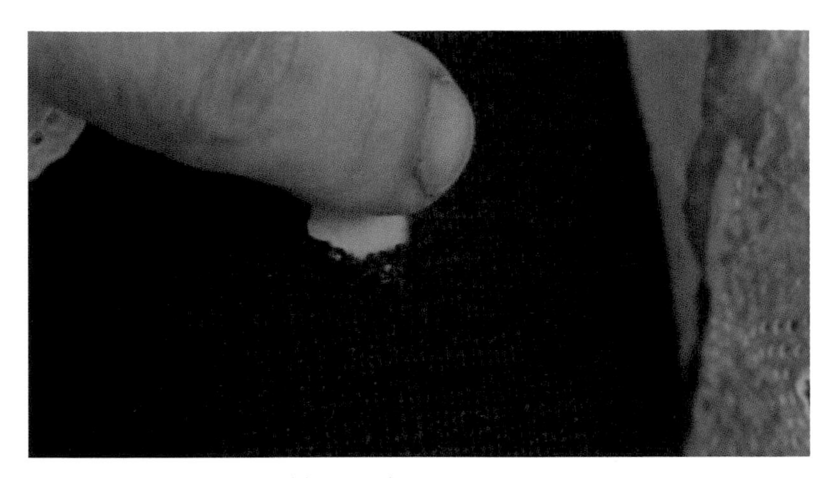

Sensual tactility (*The Piano*) (see p.32)

The male body exposed (*The Piano*, 1993) (see p.45)

"Vibrant and clashing colour" (*Peel*, 1982) (see p.64)

(above and opposite) Three successive images of entrapment (*The Portrait of a Lady*, 1996) (see p.131–2)

A much debated prologue (*The Portrait of a Lady*, 1996) (see p.128)

Characters in pools of light in darkness (*The Portrait of a Lady*, 1996) (see p.134)

Kitsch conversion (*Holy Smoke*, 1999) (see p.148)

Screwball role reversal (*Holy Smoke*, 1999) (see p.152)

Tourist imagery (*Holy Smoke*, 1999) (see p.155)

useful summary of this style, one she qualifies as 'excessive' in relation to storytelling needs:

> Imagery in *Sweetie* is excessive in its highly artificial constructions. Nothing ever looks normal or predictable. The consistent use of wide angle, deep focus and special lighting render every image strange throughout the film. The effect is again a subtle *Verfremdung* [distanciation]: the everyday world of houses, gardens and streets looks unfamiliar, almost hostile to the people who take up awkward positions within the space they occupy. ... The bizarre style converges with the irrational behaviour of the characters by deviating from Hollywood cinematic conventions. ... The film's persistent use of long shots and wide angle builds up a quality of the image that in all its artificiality can be described as the image-as-excess. These images construct a fragmented narrative that moves along in fits and starts.[19]

Take some shots from *Sweetie*. Late in the film, the heroine Kay (Karen Colston), her boyfriend Louis (Tom Lycos) and her father Gordon (Jon Darling) leave their suburban town to visit Kay's mother Flo (Dorothy Barry) in the outback at a jackaroo ranch where she has gone after separating from her husband. From this narrative development – which I hesitate to call a single sequence since so much that happens in it takes place as strange, isolated bits that don't necessarily integrate together – any number of shots signal *Sweetie*'s deliberate and relentless attempt to make things strange. In fact, it is necessary to treat many of the shots as isolated elements since an initial effect of strangeness derives from *Sweetie*'s deliberately disconnected editing pattern which generally eschews matches of action and contiguities of space to make each new image disrupt the presence of the previous one and turn the flow of shots into a vibrant clash. For example, the trip itself is rendered by means of a series of fragments even though everything is taking place in the space of one automobile: an extreme close-up of Louis sleeping (so close we don't know precisely where he is in the car); a close-up profile of Gordon driving; a view of Kay's lap and legs with her hands resting on them, the rest of her body cut off starkly by the lines of the frame; an abruptly introduced shot of Louis meditating in the foreground in the back of the car while Gordon, standing outside, watches quizzically from the background and then moves forward to rock the car; a somewhat contiguous shot of Kay watching Gordon do this, but with her body poised between weird mounds of dirt, again rendering the transition strange; and so on. Nothing really adds up here; the shots float free as if each had its own anecdotal power.

The filming of the trip to the outback is a virtual compendium of the stylistic traits that distinguish Campion's early filmic efforts and that are part of Sally Bongers's style of cinematography at the time. First, there is a play on scale in the image created through stark compositions that pit large figures in foreground against smaller ones in the background – as in a shot of a discussion by family members of how to leave Sweetie (Geneviève Lemon) behind, composed with Kay in the extreme foreground, Louis a diminutive blur in the background, and Gordon coming into frame and wandering between them, all of this accentuated by a clash between Kay's bright blue shirt and a bright red lamp behind Louis. Gordon's move into the frame suggests another aspect of this jarring mode of composition: the film frequently sets up a strange composition that it then renders even stranger by having someone move into the image in unexpected fashion and upset the established spatial relationships. Perhaps the most extreme example of this play with composition occurs in a scene just after the voyagers have reached the outback. Kay, Louis and her mother go out swimming and a boldly extravagant composition sets the camera at water level (its lapping rubbing up and down against the camera lens) and plays off Flo and then Louis paddling in the background with Kay's face floating into frame in the extreme foreground.

Sweetie also creates strangeness through insistent looks at the camera made all the more striking by an extreme closeness to the camera lens. As film scholars have long noted, the look at the camera can bring with it an uncanny effect, a violation of the gap between the fictional world on-screen and the safe place of the spectator hidden in the dark of the theatre. Not all such looks are disturbing in this way. For instance, shot/reverse-shots between two characters in conversation calm the estranging effect of the look by covering it with narrative motivation (the characters are not looking at us so much as at an in-story interlocutor that we momentarily identify with). Additionally, a scene of performance (someone playing explicitly to an audience) can easily involve direct address to the spectator without it coming off as disturbing (hence, in *A Girl's Own Story*, there is a very early shot of the girls performing a Beatles song to the camera, and the film ends with another moment of explicit performance with the song 'I feel the cold'). Likewise, there is a look at the camera in which the character's eyes seem to focus not on any object (the spectator, the camera itself) so much as appear to be looking out onto another realm of being, an imaginative realm somehow beyond the camera and the spectator (for example, the empty stare of damaged or deranged heroines in D. W. Griffith films). This is a fundamental strategy in *The Piano* in the scenes of longing we analysed earlier. Ada – and to a lesser degree, Baines – are often looking intently forward, but their look is filled with an ineffable desire that carries beyond the spectator and doesn't seem directly to assail him or her.

Sweetie does make use of some of these normalising approaches to the look at the camera – there are, for instance, dialogue scenes in shot/reverse-shot, there are moments where Kay especially looks wonderingly off-screen as if caught in reverie – but in many cases it employs a much more disturbing look. First of all, many of these looks go on for a very long time and are not easily and immediately recuperated into a narrative structure. For instance, when Kay first notices that Louis has a question mark on his forehead (a lock of hair pointing down to a mole), her frozen gaze goes on and on. Second, a number of the looks at the camera involve a character coming from the background into the foreground, a movement that again puts intense emphasis on the activity of looking. Thus, when Kay goes to the fortune teller at the beginning of the film, she moves ever closer to the camera (and it also moves forward to meet her) as she wonders about her existence. Third, the look at the camera is frequently presented as insistently directed, targeting a quite specific object of view (rather than the look into nothingness that characterises gazes of longing in *The Piano*) and thus deliberately confuses the place of the spectator and that of the object supposedly being looked at. Perhaps most striking in this respect is a look at the camera in the scene, also discussed above, of the family discussing how to go on their trip to visit Flo but leave the overbearing Sweetie behind. Sweetie has ensconced herself in the family car and is refusing to leave, but Gordon suggests they can exploit the fact that she will have to emerge at some point to relieve herself. From this declaration, we cut to a typically strikingly composed shot – Louis in the background on a couch, Kay closer to the camera – made all the more strange by garish decor and awkward body poses (Louis is upside down on the couch, Kay appears to be on her hands and knees). As an off-screen sound indicates that Sweetie is opening the car door (almost as a direct response to Gordon's optimism), Kay begins to move around the floor looking directly at the camera (which takes the place of an unseen window) and doing so from a range of positions. A point-of-view shot then shows us Sweetie kneeling by the side of the car and relieving herself. From this, we return to the previous set-up but now as Kay sits back in amazement, Gordon comes into the frame in the extreme foreground, thereby filling up the image, looks pointedly at the camera (and thereby at us) and cringes in disgust. *Sweetie* is, in many ways, an aggressive film, and one form of its assault comes from a direct address to the audience that is eerie and disturbing.

There is also an attempt to render things strange by choosing for the content of the images sights that are themselves curious or out of the ordinary (for example, the shocking sight of Sweetie squatting down to relieve herself next to the family car). Perhaps the most notable of such images comes in a whimsical moment where the film cuts to two of the jackaroo cowboys on the outback practising complicated dance moves – without any narrative preparation setting this up – and doing so in such close proximity that they appear to be spooning. Perhaps, one could find some narrative justification for the shot in some notion of Australian matesmanship (white men in the outback finding solidarity through bonding) that even verges on the homosocial (an earlier shot on the ranch has Louis and Flo discussing things in the foreground while, through an opening, we see two big jackaroos in frilly aprons doing dishes). Likewise, the film deliberately emphasises the strangeness of the jackaroos in a shot where Kay is cutting their hair: as she moves from one man to the next, a hitherto unseen dwarfish jackaroo comes surprisingly into view. In an interview published with the screenplay of *Sweetie*, Campion herself talks of the soft quirkiness in the scenes with the jackaroos: 'I wanted to make a film with likeable men. And this was a bit like Snow White and the Seven Dwarfs. Mother goes out there and these men heal her: it's a celebration of the gentle side of men. They all love their Mummies. It's adorable. The girls on the crew loved that scene: they all wanted to help select the men to play the jackaroos.'[20]

If the opening graphics of *Peel* emphasise human relationship as a triangular configuration that contains the potential for shifting allegiances; if *Passionless Moments* breaks down relationship into a series of disconnected anecdotes of random encounter; if *A Girl's Own Story* concentrates instead, as its name implies, on an overall narrative trajectory (the growth of one girl facing young adulthood), it might be said that *Sweetie* combines aspects of all of these earlier films' depictions of the vagaries of interpersonal relationship. There is, for instance, in *Sweetie* as there is in *Peel*, emphasis on the ways a few characters, especially members of a family, interact in variable (but limited) patterns in which power relations modify and alliances form and deform. Similarly, like *A Girl's Own Story* (which could also have been a title for *Sweetie*), *Sweetie* centres, within these shifting lines of relationship, on the story of one woman and the ways she tries to wend her way through the interpersonal complexities around her.

Significantly, though, this protagonist is not the title character, Sweetie, but her sister Kay. Despite the fact the title of the film might lead us to assume that the story is Sweetie's, she is introduced into the film only after about twenty-six minutes, and her entrance into the film is marked as a form of violence (literally so in that she smashes a window to get into Kay's home, metaphorically so in that her brusque arrival dramatically disrupts Kay's plans and projects to gain control of her confused life situation). Although Kay remains the central figure of the film – and narrative progress is measured by how far she has come from the story's beginning to its ending – *Sweetie* overlays Kay's tale with others that fragment her story and transform narrative into a series of often anecdotal bits.

But initially, the story is Kay's. Significantly, the film is introduced with a voice-over by her (and this personal narration returns from time to time) whereas the screenplay has no such narration. Like *A Girl's Own Story*, *Sweetie* is in large part a diaristic work of testimony in which a young woman tries to mediate a world that comes to her in anecdotal bits and pieces. For all its strangeness, *Sweetie* is also a film whose emphasis on feminine subjective experience is resonant for many viewers who can feel for Kay as she goes through typical experiences around her family and relationship.

Kay is not in full control of this narrative although this very lack of power increases sympathies with her as a victim of experience. From early in the film, the narrative and editing style of *Sweetie* relativises Kay's centrality to things, even as it encourages overall sympathy for her. Thus, if the very opening – Kay going to see a fortune teller – stays with Kay in virtually every shot, the next scene, back at the bank where Kay works, begins with Kay's complete elimination. From a cut on Kay leaving the fortune teller and wondering about meeting a man with a question mark on his forehead, there is an abrupt transition to a shot of Louis and Cheryl (a co-worker whom he has just become engaged to) kissing and other co-workers excitedly discovering the engagement ring. The scene is played out in a long-running single shot (with one quick cutaway to a close-up of the ring) and only eventually is Kay brought back into the narrative when one of the women asks if she wants to see the engagement ring. There is a cut to Kay sitting alone and caught up in her thoughts, a shot that isolates her off to one side of the frame. She responds that getting caught up in such gleeful activities is not her 'kind of thing' and then gets up and walks out of the scene, leaving the others to talk about her. When Kay returns to the communal lunch room two shots later, she continues to be excluded, being represented visually as no more than two hands that jut into frame while Louis and Cheryl confront her and make fun of her way of life. Here, two ways in which Kay undergoes exclusion are depicted, and these strategies will be consistently returned to throughout the film. On the one hand, Kay willingly separates herself off from a world that she doesn't find interesting or, in other cases, actively menaces her. On the other hand, the world of others actively works to repel Kay, to make her an outsider.

As I've suggested, a number of films directed by Jane Campion chronicle how people plot to control others through conspiracy, private negotiation and so on. Characters are talked about behind their backs and find that these conversations can have intense consequences for their future. Throughout *Sweetie*, Kay, as well as Sweetie, will be the object of other people's deliberations and machinations – from the co-workers mocking her in this early scene; to Melanie, a woman friend of Louis's, trying to help him with his sexual problems with Kay by giving him a book on tantric sex (when Kay discovers that there has been talk behind her back about her relationship with Louis, she reacts with great anger, qualifying Melanie as 'such a bitch'); to Louis planting a symbolic tree without her permission; to Louis and Sweetie trying to work things out in the household while keeping Kay out of the loop. Kay's hold on things is never more than partial, and her presence in the film is never total. In an illuminating detail, *Sweetie* offers the converse of an image that runs through *The Piano*. The later film has numerous shots in which Ada and Flora move in unison and engage in the same gestures (for example, when they come to implore Baines to take them back to *The Piano* on the beach) in a way that implies a vital community of women (one that Baines is curious about and feels excluded from). In contrast, *Sweetie* has no affirmative images of women acting in unison (indeed, Sweetie and Kay are figures in conflict, never in collusion) and substitutes instead a sardonic shot in which Kay's co-workers stand in the background of the frame and mimic her as she twirls her hair. Visually, Kay is separated off from the co-workers, existing in another plane from them, and narratively, it is made clear that behind her back, Kay's co-workers have nothing but shared disdain for her. (Likewise, in a later scene, there is a cross-cutting between Kay caught outside in the wind and the co-workers watching her from a window and commenting cruelly on her misfortune.)

To be sure, Kay frequently is an active agent of her own fate – from deciding to visit a psychic to using the prediction as justification for conspiring with Louis to take him away from Cheryl. But she is just as frequently a figure who seems victimised by the ways of the world. Obviously, the arrival of her disturbed if not psychotic sister, Sweetie, manifests an extreme case of Kay's vulnerability and her powerlessness. Kay may be a narrator but all that she can narrate is her own relativity: thus, her opening narration tells how, when young, her sister had a tree house built for her and how Kay was not allowed into it, resulting in her ongoing morbid fear of trees. As the film's title reminds us, Kay is not the only important figure in the film's narrative universe.

Kay's sister Sweetie is a force both of disorganisation and reorganisation for the film's narrative. On the one hand, starting with the very fact that her name titles the film even though the story appears to be Kay's, Sweetie's abrupt arrival into the film breaks the narrative flow, sending it in directions that are unpredictable (both for other characters in the film and for the spectator) and fragmenting it into ever weirder, ever more bizarre situations. On the other hand, Sweetie also figures as a veritable contagion whose presence obliges others to gravitate around her, to have their lives determined by her. An inescapable, overbearing force who sows pandemonium wherever she turns, Sweetie makes narratives bend to her will. Sweetie is a figure who appropriates and consumes the world around her (literally so in her endless ingestion of things, including her sister's collection of ceramic horses). If human relationships are seen to be ever shifting, ever vulnerable to changes of commitment and alliance, bit by bit we discover that it is so for the characters in this film because Sweetie has virtually sown the seeds of discord and disunity into the very being of these characters. Even as these characters try to move forward with lives they believe are their own, they find their ability to project themselves freely into the future predetermined by Sweetie's overriding story. Indeed, even before she reappears in the characters' lives, it is apparent that she has been present to them as a force they would like to repress but which festers inside them. Not for nothing does the opening of the film chronicle both Kay's attempts to take control of her life by going to the psychic for direction and the extent to which her life has been determined by the attention given to her sister which she has internalised as phobia and superstition.

In many ways, for example, Sweetie's family members have been blocked psychologically by her hold over them. Sweetie herself has been arrested by the image of a childhood stardom (which she imagines she had but which the film reveals to be an empty illusion) that she obsessively returns to and tries to recapture and, most important of all, insists that her family and acquaintances share with her. One long take, for instance, has Sweetie begging her father Gordon to help her to show off her prize performance piece to Kay's boyfriend Louis: Gordon finally gives in to Sweetie's whiny imploring and we discover that Sweetie's talent, such as it is, consists of standing on a chair and tipping it over to the ground without her falling over. Sweetie is a regressive figure who keeps cycling back to infantile dreams, but her power is such that she gets others to participate, willingly or not, in this regression. Perhaps the most extreme moment of Sweetie's overbearing mode of theatricality that obsessively requires the unflagging attention of those around her is the long sequence in which she goes back up into the tree house of her childhood. There, any sense of stylish performance is left behind as Sweetie regresses to a veritable animality and becomes a pure force of corporeal play given over to taunts, tantrums, farts, slobberings and so on. Sweetie becomes an intense object of attention on the part of family and neighbours even as she repulses them and pushes their patience to the limit.

Sweetie's contagiousness is so strong that she continues to exert an influence even after her death. Although Kay does seem by the film's end to be turning Sweetie's passing into a positive potential to get beyond psychical blocks (Kay had been turned off from sex with her boyfriend but now seems ready to rediscover a sexual relationship), Gordon in contrast seems ever more to have sunk into Sweetie's obsessions. The last scene has him seeing an image of the childhood Sweetie in princess outfit crooning a love song to him (at one point earlier in the film, there was a strong hint of something sexual between Sweetie and her father).

Sweetie's tension between fragmentation and narrative progress – whether that of characters as they try to determine their own lives or that of Sweetie herself who comes to organise all lives around hers – contributes to its role as an art film, one whose complexities inevitably would divide audiences (as it did at Cannes). *Sweetie* does not offer typically mainstream appeals. On the one hand, there's a kind of insistent and even claustrophobic quality of reduction and simplification to the film that makes it approach the gruelling experience of certain works of sparse, even barren minimalism (for example, the plays of Samuel Beckett). Like a theatre piece in which a limited group of characters revolve around each other in the traps of their lives, *Sweetie* deals with a very few figures in a circumscribed world (in a small but nice detail, Kay and Louis are always having to hide in

Fantasy images

their own home because the gregarious next-door neighbour child Clayton is, like Sweetie, always imploring them to watch his feats and play his games) and then it has Sweetie's entrance onto the scene circumscribe things even further. Once Sweetie appears, everything gravitates around her – the characters, the narrative, the viewer's attention – and it is as if there has been a funnelling in of the film's narrative world.

While *Sweetie* can often be wildly funny, it can also be an intensely painful film to watch, especially in the inescapable and insistent shrillness of Sweetie who so dominates the space around her. This again accounts for some of the art-film status of *Sweetie*: like the most transgressive, assaultive and difficult works, *Sweetie* is pushing the envelope of watchability, displaying in its frame a painfully unbearable figure who works less to move the narrative forward than to freeze it in a relentless minimalism of growls, harsh cries, screams and suchlike. This is why the sequence I described earlier of the family fleeing Sweetie to visit Kay's mother out in the country has such a feel of exhilaration and openness to it: for a time, the characters are once again able to live their own lives, free for a while of the influence of Sweetie, and they can commune with the elements (the scene of Kay and her mother swimming) and give in to effusive and affirmative expressions of personal joy through activities such as singing and dancing. Even more important, it is away from Sweetie that Gordon and his wife can reconcile and begin their relationship anew. Obviously, though, the film depicts such moments of liberation as fleeting interludes: Sweetie is inescapable and the family members will be forced back into her world.

On the other hand, just as Sweetie's story disrupts Kay's – even if it then sucks in Kay's narrative to make it come under Sweetie's sway – *Sweetie* is a film that endlessly shakes up its minimalist universe by the addition of new elements. This is both an insistently claustrophobic world in which so much of human action and interaction seems closed off and predetermined *and* one open to chance, random event, digression, anecdote. Where the minimalism constructs a hyper-reality in which, for instance, the space of the home circumscribes human potential and insists on its inescapable presence over the lives of characters, there is also in *Sweetie* a *surreality* in which the film can shift beyond present space and present narrative to offer glimpses of other meanings and other modes of being. First of all, there are quite obvious digressions in which dreams and fantasies interrupt the flow of narrative through frenetic montage in which disconnected images swirl up and take over the screen. Second, there are the larger shifts in narrative – like the abrupt switch from Kay's story to that of the film's title character – that are unpredictable and equally disruptive. Third, there is a continued emphasis on accident and random event. Thus, if one of the ways Kay tries to control her life is by going to a psychic (where already there's a strong dose of surreality through the presence of the psychic's handicapped relative who, *à la* David Lynch, drools, babbles and convulses through the scenes of Kay's visits), the lesson she will draw from this is of the quirky randomness of life. She is told she will have a relationship with a man with a question mark on his forehead, and this will lead her to seduce fellow worker Louis on whom a tousled lock of hair points down to a mole to form the mark of interrogation that Kay is seeking. To be sure, from this crazy beginning, Kay and Louis are able indeed to build up a relationship (one that by the film's end seems ready to endure), but the film treats the seeming realisation of the psychic's prophecy with sardonic and satiric derision (for example, the music is wildly overdone) and emphasises the accidental, artificial nature of human relationships. Life here does not naturally and logically organise itself into a coherent narrative but is dominated rather by illogic, by a sense of the arbitrary.

In light of my discussion of *The Piano* as a late version of the female

Gothic film, it is intriguing to note that Anneke Smelik argues in her analysis that *Sweetie* is readable also as a work within that tradition. Here, she regards *Sweetie* in light of feminist theorist Tania Modleski's early work (in *Loving with a Vengeance: Mass-Produced Fantasies for Women*, 1979) on the female Gothic tradition in literature. Modleski had suggested that the Gothic heroine bore a complex and often fraught emotional relationship not only with a complex, even conflicted and divided masculinity but also with an equally complicated femininity represented by another woman that the Gothic hero seems to be fixated on (for example, in *Rebecca*, the never-named heroine fears that her husband prefers the now dead Rebecca, the first Mrs de Winter, to her). Noting that *Sweetie* shares other defining features of the Gothic tradition – for instance, the emphasis on a vulnerable female protagonist who wanders through a domestic space she fears might turn against her – Smelik suggests that, for heroine Kay, her sister Sweetie comes to take up the role of this other woman. Kay initially holds out the hope that she will be the one to captivate the people in her life, but increasingly she comes to fear that Sweetie, a veritable force from the past, is the figure that others actually invest their emotions in.

Where Kay had originally seemed to be quite self-willed in her determination to realise the prophecy and win over Louis (who at that point is engaged to another woman), her discovery that Sweetie is the real captivating and controlling force leads Kay into a form of passivity, a cutting off from all emotional bond and a withdrawal into the interiority of the self (like Lorraine at the end of *After Hours*, the adults at the end of *Peel*, the girls feeling the cold in the void of *A Girl's Own Story*, or later like Ada floating in the watery grave). As Smelik notes, the Gothic situation, the sense that interpersonal space is a geography fraught with menace and risk of annihilation leads Kay to ever more deeply feel the constrictions of her situation to such a degree that no place appears to hold solace for her (although she opens up a bit in the free space of the countryside where she can swim and dance away from Sweetie's influence). After a while, neither the space of the home nor the bountiful world of nature can offer positive support to Kay. In Smelik's words, the film opposes 'the menace of uncontrolled plant life [the trees that Kay fears and has phobic nightmares about] to the sterile suffocation of suburban living', finding neither to represent something affirmative for Kay. As Smelik also notes,

> In her effort to prevent these 'hidden powers' of roots from making an appearance in broad daylight, Kay kills the whole plant. … [S]he tries to allay the hidden powers of her unconscious from emerging. Yet, in trying to keep the unconscious 'under,' as it were, she stops the process of life. Growth is then no longer possible, as indicated in her vision which equates the planting of a tree with burying the dead. Considering the above, it comes as no surprise that the relationship between Kay and Louis soon begins to show signs of wear.[21]

But just as *The Piano* follows the Gothic tradition in having Ada overcome the blockages of the past and reject primal and regressive attachment (to her piano and to her daughter as well) for the sake of a progressive and affirmative adult heterosexual relationship, so too it might seem that *Sweetie* imagines that its heroine can escape the entrapments of space and situation once there is no need to fixate on the past. At the end of the film, with Sweetie gone, Kay can move on with her life, which in this case means accepting the need for a full sexual life with Louis. Indeed, if *The Piano* fuelled erotic fantasy by presenting the possibility of a sensitive male growing out from within a stunted and stunting Gothic universe, *Sweetie* also ultimately can be seen to affirm its image of a caring masculinity. Indeed, Kay's growing fear of sex with him seems to come largely from her own psychoses, and it is easy for the spectator to feel impatient with Kay's rejection of Louis for much of the film. Kay's return to Louis can come across, then, as a positive step in her repossession of her life. In Smelik's words,

> Now that she [Kay] has lived through experiences of uncanniness and has dared to face abjection; now that she has tried to confront what she has magically tried to repress; only now can she live again. She has understood that life goes on through death. Back home, Louis has returned to her after a short break in their relationship. In one of the last images, in an obtuse angle, through the door opening, we see their feet on the bed touching.[22]

To a large degree, this form of heterosexual relationship is valorised as one force of stability in a crazy, chaotic universe.

But it would be hard to imagine that the appeal of *Sweetie* for its spectators lies primarily in its depiction of heterosexual romance. If *The Piano* could be seen by many commentators as feminist in its uplifting celebration of a woman's self-determination in the arena of the erotic, *Sweetie* is generally an unromantic film. Virtually the only moment that represents romantic love as sensual is an early one in which Kay lounges languorously and triumphantly after she and Louis have slept together for the first time, but this quick moment of bliss quickly gives way to a situation of bad luck ('Thirteen months later' a title tells us) centred on the falling apart of Louis's and Kay's romance. Throughout the film, sexual expression is either muted – it is noteworthy that the last scene represents the reconciled Louis and Kay only as disconnected legs tentatively touching each other – or treated as something fragile and furtive (Kay and Louis frantically kissing under a car as they try to hide from Cheryl); or rendered as an overly physical, even crass activity that approaches a level of disgust. Louis, for instance, can manifest his sexual desire only in ways that inspire revulsion on Kay's part (he tries to lick his way up her body and she tells him it's cold and clammy). Indeed, the most direct representation of sexual activity in the film comes when Sweetie and her producer-boyfriend have noisy, vulgar sex in the next room and prevent Louis and Kay from sleeping and going to the bathroom (with an additional confirmation of the revulsion Louis's sexuality has come to represent for Kay coming from the fact that hearing the lovemaking through the walls ends up turning Louis on). In fact, Sweetie's own extreme sexual behaviour is responsible in large part for Louis turning to increasingly unattractive and even reprehensible forms of sexual expression: he tries to lick Kay after Sweetie has come on to him (she offers to lick him all over) and his failures to excite Kay lead him to try to force himself on her in a manner that could easily qualify as rape.

If, to follow Anneke Smelik's argument, *Sweetie* is to be considered in relation to a Gothic tradition, it must be recognised that the film doesn't invest in the emphasis of one part of that tradition on the woman saved by a heroic male figure. It is Gothic rather in its concern for a woman who has to act on and against the fears she has in negotiating a dark world around her. For all his softness, Louis is no Gothic hero. On the one hand, he is as much the cause of Kay's anxieties as a solution to them. On the other hand, when Kay reveals the extent of her new-found antipathy to sexuality, Louis can offer little solace – quite the contrary, he tries all the more to force himself on Kay in ways that repel her – and little in the way of tempting eroticism. Instead, Louis falls himself into ineffectual passivity and becomes a figure with little agency. Louis indeed is an extreme version of Campion's feminised men, caught in inactive or reactive brooding, letting obsessions get the better of them, sinking into despair. Louis accomplishes very little in the film: significantly, he is not present in the penultimate scene where Kay and her family try to get Sweetie out of the tree house she has ensconced herself in.

Sweetie represents a very different form of women's cinema than *The Piano*. Both depict women's struggles for self-determination and expression, but *Sweetie* represents heterosexual romance as only one of the many life experiences a woman might confront (as important as romance is the weight of the familial past, something only hinted at in *The Piano*'s quick reference to Ada's father). If *The Piano* makes romance the primary (and primal) force of redemption, *Sweetie* suggests an irrelevance of romantic practice (irrelevant in the ways it comes about, irrelevant for the little it accomplishes). In this respect, it anticipates Campion's next film, *An Angel at My Table*, which eschews both romantic trappings and garish style to recount in subdued fashion a narrative of feminine self-determination.

An Angel at My Table (1990)

Although *Sweetie* takes up an attitude of often sardonic distance from its subject matter and undercuts the erotic component of relationship while *The Piano* approaches its subject with lush tactile proximity, both films end with heterosexual relationships and suggest this will be a new path for its heroine. Quite different in its depiction of femininity, then, is the film that separates these two works, *An Angel at My Table*. Funded by the New Zealand Film Commission, Television New Zealand, the Australian Broadcasting Corporation and Channel Four Films, *An Angel at My Table* was originally shot as a three-part television series but cut down slightly for cinematic release. The film chronicles the needs of its heroine to be free of all direction by the will of other people, including that of men as sexual partners. Certainly, as the narrative of a woman who felt trapped and, at one point in her life, was in fact literally incarcerated in the space of a psychiatric ward, *An Angel at My Table* bears resemblance to the Gothic tradition with its emphasis on a woman caught in malevolent spaces. However, where the classic Gothic film uses a redeemed masculinity to imagine a romantic salvation that sweeps in to rescue the woman from Gothic dread, *An Angel at My Table* offers little image of uplifting heterosexual romance by means of a heroic male figure. The New Zealand college professor Janet has a crush on is instrumental in having her committed to a psychiatric ward and the American university teacher she finally does have an affair with is obviously lacking in all sensitivity and can make no commitment to her.

Indeed, if *Angel* shows Janet's first sexual experience as part of a languorous and seductive idyllic image of Italy, it does so only to then deflate such romantic dreams by suggesting that, for Janet, erotic attachment can only occur in the utopian space of a passing moment in a world apart. Like the first part of the film (which I'll be discussing a little later), the Italy section of *An Angel at My Table* is handled as a series of discrete events or anecdotes as much as an integrated narrative, and this allows for the treatment of the romantic adventure as little more than one interlude, one more learning experience that Janet accumulates on her way to a larger life-narrative and lesson.

The unromantic male

The few details the film assembles about Bernard, the American history professor and would-be poet that she has an affair with, rob him of any romantic aura. Unlike, say, Harvey Keitel in *The Piano*, he is not given much presence, filmed generally in long shots that give him little visual force. Throughout, Bernard is presented as a self-centred creep and a jokester who has trouble taking things seriously (including, obviously, romantic attachment), and his encounter with Janet is bereft of romantic sentiment. For instance, as Janet and Bernard begin to make love for the first time, he keeps interrupting their efforts to vainly try out his poetry. As Janet's voiceover comments bitterly after she's been abandoned by Bernard, 'True romance, indeed. So much for poetry and music.' The romantic entanglement with Bernard is soon effaced as a formative moment in Janet's trajectory: returning to London, she affirms that she is still 'fancy free' and soon, through an abortion, expunges the last traces of her sexual encounter. If any notion of romance could be said to be an integral part of Janet's life, it is so only to the extent that, as the authors of a reference guide to New Zealand films put it, she has a 'love affair with language'.[23]

As in the romantic film, the hesitant, stumbling heroine of *An Angel at My Table* learns to grow up and project herself with self-will into a future that she is making her own. But the film emphatically portrays such a growth for Janet as occurring in the realm of words – a private connection

Isolation

between writer and page, rather than a social or sexual one with other people. The romantic heroine must learn to grow into sociality – in particular, the sociality of relationship with a man – but Janet ventures ever more into the interiority of her own imagination. If the very first narrative action of the film has the young Janet trying to buy the friendship of her classmates by stealing money to buy chewing gum for them, she will progressively learn to depend on herself, and not others. Bit by bit, she is cut off from the people around her – both unwillingly as when her father dies, and willingly as when she takes it upon herself to leave the shelter of the elderly writer Frank and venture out into a literary odyssey on her own.

The very ending of the trilogy offers a concise rendition of Janet's new-found relation to career and to sociality. Here, Janet has taken up residence in a small trailer behind her sister's house and spends her time writing. On the one hand, she cannot fully cut herself off from contact with others (as she learnt in the previous scene when reporters came to seek her out for her new-found notoriety as one of New Zealand's top writers). On the other hand, she can now deal with sociality on her own terms, according to her own desires. Janet types on her manuscript, then interrupts her activity to go outside and do the twist alone in the night (the sequence had begun with her niece seen doing the twist through the door of Janet's trailer), then interrupts that activity to return to the trailer and happily resume her writing.

Last shot of the film: Janet viewed in her writing life

Throughout much of *An Angel at My Table*, Janet is presented as someone who peeks on with envy at ways of life she is excluded from. But in this very end moment, there are significant differences from these earlier representations of Janet as a figure of repressed and thwarted longing. First, the niece is not specifically being seen from Janet's point of view (she is busy working on her manuscript and assures her sister that the niece's dancing doesn't disturb her in her craft). Second, even if Janet's twisting does suggest an enduring envy to participate in some of the activities of others, she wilfully breaks away from this activity to return to her real work of commitment. She is now what the title of Part 3 of the film calls 'The Envoy from Mirror City', which Janet Frame's autobiography makes clear (perhaps more so than the film) is intended to describe the ways in which the writer's mission is to go into a space of imagination (the city that is a mirror of our own) and bring news of its beauties back to the real world. Imagination creates parallel geographies that poets can report on.

It fits this theme that the structure of Janet's actions in the last segment sandwiches the moment of dancing alone and of having just chatted with her sister between two scenes of Janet caught up in her writing. Worldly activity, sociality, envy of the life of others, are now relative experiences, little more than interludes surpassed by the life of artistic creation and potentially serving as raw material for imaginative transformation through writing (as, in fact, the things we see Janet live through on-screen will become elements in her own written autobiography). It's an appropriate touch, then, that the last image – Janet alone at her typewriter – is presented through the window of the trailer with the camera and the spectator peering in on her. For much of the film, Janet has been either a passive object for others to look at with designs to shaping her according to their own purposes or a passive subject who peeks in enviously at the lives of others from a safe but powerless position of voyeurism. In the last shot, it is now Janet who is peeked in on: she has found her niche and become a full subject in her own right, a figure to be looked at with respect and admiration (just as in the previous scene the journalists had shown unambiguous and non-condescending regard for her).

One way to understand how far Janet has come in the narrative of *An*

Life as a series of anecdotes

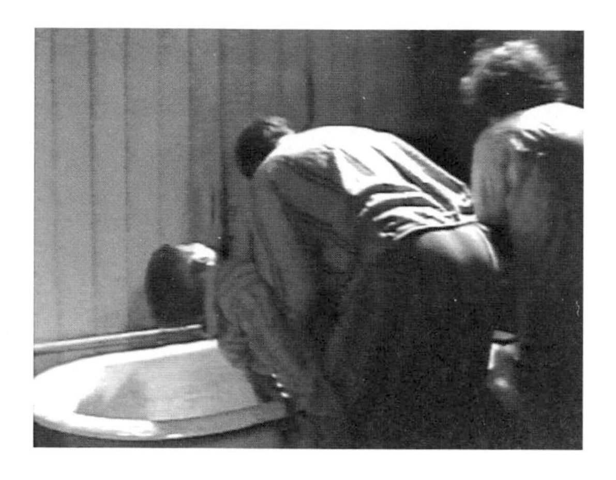

Angel at My Table is to compare its resolute image of Janet the writer to the much more hesitant attitude towards cultural activity shown in the first section of the film. Much of Part 1 of the film is offered as a succession of little bits of life (in interviews, Campion says that the idea was to capture childhood memory as a series of fragments). There is, to be sure, a narrative line here: Janet grows up. It is revealing in this respect that the use of three different actresses to play Janet at different stages of her life occurs within this first part (rather than being distributed through the three parts), emphasising how much the first section of the film is about growing up. But this insistence on Janet's individual process of maturation is presented as interacting with no one overarching narrative line in the world around her. The world around Janet is endlessly unpredictable, endlessly coming at her as a series of fragments that she watches and tries to assimilate.

There is no necessary unity to these anecdotes (for example, the few scenes dealing with Janet's epileptic brother do not add up to a narrative and have little consequence other than to suggest one more dimension to Janet's home life). But there are some recurrent kinds of event in the first part, and there are resonances across the narrative between individual anecdotes. In particular, many of the anecdotes in Part 1 have to do with kinds of fictionalising. Starting with the first narrative action – in which young Janet steals money to buy chewing gum and lies to her teacher about it – *An Angel at My*

Performance

Table's first part chronicles an array of forms of play-acting, of story-making, of performance and of fiction-making. There are literal acts of theatricalising and of performing: a school audition for a play; Janet's sister Myrtle's performance on the radio; young Janet's reading of her own poem to her class; a classmate's effusive singing; Jane Campion's mother playing a rhetorically effusive teacher of poetry; and so on. But there is also a more diffuse sense in this first part of acting and fictionalising as something that suffuses everyday behaviour rather than just appearing on special occasions. Young Janet's world, for instance, is one in which people are endlessly theatricalising and where forms of performance, both professional and everyday, are presented to others for their approval. Performance is one way for the working-class people in the film to add artistry to their existence and be noticed by others. For instance, when the Frame girls first make the acquaintance of a neighbourhood child, she immediately asks them if they want to see her Spanish dance and a cross-cutting links her performance to the girls' applause. This new-found friend, in fact, unleashes a new level of performance in the Frame girls (who have always been quite theatrical, as we see), as her aristocratic manner (however fake) impels the other girls to preen and prance and attempt to adopt new images for themselves. (The last time Janet sees her sister Myrtle alive, the latter is play-acting with overdone gestures.)

As this example shows, moments of theatricality and performance in Part 1 of *An Angel at My Table* serve to inspire others to emulate and imitate. Janet and her cohort continually take the play-acting of others as a source for their own fictionalising activities. They view someone's act and then have to do it themselves. No scene indicates this more directly than one in which Janet, having won a library card as a school prize, brings home books for the whole family: a close-up on fairy-tale images from one of the volumes cuts to a misty, poetic shot of the Frame children out in the moonlight acting out the image they have seen. Significantly, this scene of a book's inspiration immediately precedes the transition from child Janet to adolescent Janet and announces a new section that begins with Janet reading about some poems of hers that have been published in a newspaper.

Janet's own access to the world of fiction has its limits in the first part of

Game playing at the expense of authority

the film. While Janet herself is a fictionaliser (as we see in her lie-telling in the first sequence), she quickly learns that not all activities of creation are equally worthy, are equally effective, are equally open to her. Take, for instance, a scene with another working-class child, Poppy, whom Janet has befriended. The two girls play at a game of empowering reversal of teacher–student domination wherein they line up a series of bottles that they treat as recalcitrant school-children to be punished physically. The scene of Poppy and Janet meeting for the first time and then playing at their game follows one in which Janet and a few other students are singled out by school officials because of health or hygiene problems (a scene in which the students are described and carefully catalogued); Janet and Poppy's game, then, is an act of resistance against forces of authority (resistance of the sort that the older Janet cannot marshal later on when alone in the hospital and undergoing debilitating treatment). But this idyllic game-playing at the expense of the educational system and the placing of Janet on the same footing as another child in carnivalising worldly power structures is a momentary, vulnerable event. After using a vulgarism she learnt from Poppy in front of her parents, Janet is banned from speaking to her friend ever again. She is, from early on, a figure of solitude who rarely finds a full sharing with other people. Significantly, when Janet and Poppy next have a short encounter, a few years later, it is Poppy who is the performer and

Janet once again is in the position of audience member, listening to Poppy recite a poem she has had to memorise at school.

Indeed, in many of Janet's encounters with the world of fictionalising and performance in the first part of the film, she is placed in the position of passive observer, reduced to envy of an imaginative realm she feels excluded from. For instance, in one sequence (immediately following the last encounter of Janet and Poppy), the adolescent Janet looks on as a teacher affectionately chides another student, Shirley, for not listening to class lessons since she is such a dreamer, 'always lost', as the teacher says, 'in the world of your poetic imagination'. Janet looks on wistfully, evidently wishing she could be deemed a dreamer, a person of imagination, too. (In Frame's autobiography, the envy is rendered even more explicit: young Janet felt it was she who really deserved the teacher's admiration.) The next sequence has dreamer Shirley singing poetically in class as Janet listens on raptly, her envy augmented when she overhears another student saying that Shirley has recently lost her father. As Janet Frame's autobiography makes clear, Janet felt deprived of the great tragedies of life that others could turn into heartfelt inspirations for artistry and emotional expression. The sequence of Shirley singing is immediately followed by a shot of Janet dreamily looking into a mirror and then mockingly imitating Shirley's pretentious fluttering of her head, her quivering, her emotive rolling of the eyes. Janet both desires the world of imagination that others seem to possess while desiring it in her own terms. Not for nothing is she declaring soon afterwards in a voice-over that she has decided not to become a teacher but a writer.

But to assume a consistent role and power of imagination for herself, Janet will have to learn several things about creative activity. First, as the film's opening sequence bears out, a performance for purposes of deceiving others (the lie about the gum) is an improper and unappreciated form of fictionalising. Second, Janet will have to learn that the act of fictionalising is a supreme activity, a serious commitment of self that cannot be entered into lightly. Thus, one early form of performance comes in the guise of game-playing. To take two small examples, a very early shot has Janet's brother playing at being an Indian on the warpath; a later scene has Janet and her siblings all in bed playing a seemingly endless game of turning in one direction and the other in unison. As she grows Janet will learn to put such frivolity behind her and realise that if writing is a fictionalising, it is not a game. Third, Janet will have to fight with the world around her for her right to be a writer. Thus, in an early scene, the young Janet will be assigned to write a poem for class; when her sister Myrtle sees her writing the line 'evening shadows touch the sky' she demands that Janet change the line to 'tint the sky' since that, she declares, is what is required in poetry. But, in a nice touch, when we see Janet reading the poem in class, it once again says 'touch the sky', suggesting an insistence, no matter how minor, on having her own way with her writing.

Janet will have to learn that, until she assumes control of her own creative life, whatever her own will and decision about creative commitment, her own personal ambition can come crashing up against the vagaries of an outside world that will not always fall into step with her desire. Thus, while Janet can make a sort of declaration of independence in stating that writing will be her avocation, this is still a career path she must hide from her family. And the scene of declaration is immediately followed by one of Janet getting her first period; whatever her artistic ambition, the flight of imagination is brought back to earth by inescapable qualities of body and materiality. With her eccentric hair, her rotting teeth, and her vulnerability to mental illness, Janet's creative powers of artistic self-invention are for the first parts of the film bound to earthly limitation.

But as the last section of the film bears out in its contrast between earthly voyage (Janet travelling to Europe and having vivid experiences) and the force of imagination (the 'Mirror City'), the solution for Janet is not so much to change the givens of her physical situation (although she does repair some ills such as her teeth) as to realise a new way to live in the world. In several interviews, Jane Campion has talked of the difficulties in filming the writing life (how to avoid clichés of the writer at his or her work feverishly searching for the right word?). It seems to me that *An Angel at My Table* constructs its affirmative image of a full commitment to writing by distinguishing between the worldly narratives Janet finds herself in and the narrative of interiority and imagination.

On the one hand, there are all the things that happen to Janet, including events of great and immediate consequence such as her incarceration in the asylum with its horrific treatments. We might note even how great historical events (of which in any case there are few in the film) are de-dramatised by being represented as mere coincidences that Janet happens to glimpse from an outsider position: for example, the adolescent Janet watching her dad prepare for military service at the outbreak of the Second World War; the end of the war shown through people happily going off to celebrate while Janet looks on in her exclusion. On the other hand, even the worst of experiences – the illness, the death of family members, the traumas of self-doubt – are intellectualised as memories (after all, what we are seeing is supposed to be a visualisation of Janet Frame's memoirs), turned into inspirational material for aesthetic and imaginative reconstruction.

To be sure, the incarceration – which is the centrepiece of the film – is an intensely visceral experience in which we see all the force of medical power played out on Janet's body in torturous fashion. Undoubtedly, the film is commonly thought of as about a woman writer who was in the asylum and only got out by chance. Undoubtedly, the real Janet Frame is thought of this way too. But I would contend that the film downplays the consequential effect of the horrendous medical treatment. It is one more ordeal that Janet has to go through in order to put it behind her and build on it imaginatively (as when a friendly doctor tells her later on to write about her time in hospital). By the third part of the film, certainly, Janet has discovered a resilience and self-reliance that indeed enable her to put the past, including the past of mental illness, in perspective. The discovery that much of her malady was caused by the very treatment itself offers her an intellectual release from, and transcendence of, the physical facts and effects of terrible and misapplied medical treatment.

The film ultimately is able to downplay momentous occurrences in the physical world. (It might even matter that the most physical change in the film – from one actress playing Janet to the next – occurs fully in the first section of the film, leaving one actress playing Janet through the last two parts.) While the incarceration is an intensely dramatic moment of the film – albeit an exceptional and ultimately surmounted one – much of the film works through a systematic de-dramatisation of events. Despite its temporal scope (a film lasting over two hours that covers years in a life) and despite its geographic sweep (journeys all over New Zealand and then to Europe and finally back home), there's a marked modesty to *An Angel at My Table*. This is first of all the modesty of Janet's story which despite momentous events – the drowning death of two sisters, years of misguided and terrifyingly painful medical treatment – is finally about someone discovering the simple vocation of writer (hence, the need for the 'cliché' of the writer disconnected from the rest of the world and reduced to direct contact with the typewriter). But there is also a modesty in the ways the film depicts Janet's trajectory.

Indeed, for all its seemingly broad move through a variety of locales, *An Angel at My Table* seems resolutely un-epic in look. For example, despite the sense of triumphant liberation and independence it entails, much of Janet's trip to Europe is de-dramatised. Janet's time in Paris, for instance, is reduced telegraphically to six short, understated shots that either have veritably stereotypical status (thus, the first shot is of the Eiffel Tower seen through a mist) or centre more on Janet than on the city (thus, the longest shot of the sequence focuses entirely on Janet looking out from her hotel room at a city that remains resolutely off-screen). For all its lush romanticism, Paris is a transitory place that both Janet and the film quickly pass through.

Tourist stereotypes

The modesty of the film is primarily stylistic: this is a film with few of the garish, quirky flashes (for example, weirdly estranging compositions) that distinguish previous Campion films. *An Angel at My Table* is a film of relative visual sobriety. For example, it makes frequent use of close shots and thereby eschews the jarring or playful compositional patterns of the earlier works since there is little space in the tighter frame for such contrasts to be set up. Significantly, at the same time, few of these close shots are extremely close and thereby they avoid the distortions, so exploited in the earlier works, that occur when objects (such as faces) are overly close to the camera lens. The rare cases of such distortion – as when the face of Janet's teacher looms up grotesquely and frightfully when she punishes Janet for stealing money to buy chewing gum for her classmates – are virtually all given psychological justification (this is Janet's subjective perception of things), rather than attributed to an ironic perspective from the film itself.

Some commentators have noted in fact that Sally Bongers was not chosen as director of photography for *An Angel at My Table* and therefore could not contribute her distinctive style of filming. In interviews, Campion also suggests that the need for a sober look to the film derived from a desire to defer to the real Janet Frame and the integrity of her own story and not detract from its depiction by the interference of a flamboyant cinematic style. Additionally, Campion has suggested that the need to be modest and to eschew epic ambitions came from the fact that *An Angel at My Table* was originally designed as a work for television with its ostensible need for simplicity and intimacy (however, it should perhaps be noted that the history of television is filled with attempts at epic narration: *Masada* (1981), *North and South* (1985), *V* (1983), various biblical extravaganzas and so on).

Instead of offering a larger scope, *An Angel at My Table* hones in on Janet, making her an often immobile centre of space, rather than a figure who moves actively and energetically through the world. Certainly, each of the film's parts begins with an image of physical motion – from a baby's stumbling walk in the first to Janet coming to the city to begin college in the second to her leaving for Europe in the third. But the activity of movement is in each case limited primarily to the opening of these three parts: after a moment of movement, Janet comes to take up residence in a space that she will try to act upon and that will act upon her. The real journey of growth she engages in is an internalised one. As Sue Gillett puts it, in one of the rare analyses of the film, 'The spaces traversed by Janet are created in the film as spaces which Janet defines. Typically, they are not huge, romantic, exotic, panoramic, but, more often they are intimate. It is as if the camera operates to create "manageable" relations between the female artist and her external environments.'[24] Significantly, for all the physical movement of the film from its very first shots on (where we see the Frame family moving by train to a new home), the overall narrative trajectory of the film works as a circular form in which Janet comes back to where she started from. Every place away from New Zealand is only a transitory step on a voyage back home. Towards the end of the film, Janet's father dies and she returns to the family homestead. In a revealing anecdote, she tries on his shoes with evident delight. Janet has reconciled herself to her life, put her family history in perspective while demarcating her own identity from it, and found ways to make domestic space her own. The voyage out has only been a means for Janet to be able to resume life in her country of origin.

With a few exceptions, *An Angel at My Table* includes Janet in virtually every scene, making this a story filtered through her, a story that matters insofar as it affects her directly and personally. In many scenes of the film, events happen around Janet, and such moments are specifically represented

The return home: trying on dad's shoes

Peeking in on the world

through Janet looking in on them. She is frequently in a space adjacent to the unfolding of actions and peeks at them through a window or a doorway or from a relative distance: for instance, the very young Janet peering out from a train window to see the town of Seacliff, location of an insane asylum (that the adult Janet will end up in); Janet (and her siblings) watching her parents try to deal, late at night, with their son's epileptic seizure; Janet and a friend watching Janet's sister Myrtle trying to make love with a boy; Janet in bed watching the shadows cast by a fight between her parents; Janet watching Myrtle going off to the baths (where she will accidentally drown); Janet at Seacliff looking furtively through a window at the victims of the lobotomy she is also threatened with; and so on. In some cases, Janet's acts of looking are impelled by curiosity – just what are these events going on around her? – but envy for a world not hers also seems to be the driving force behind some of her glances or glazes. Frequently, Janet looks on longingly at a world she knows she cannot possess. For instance, she sits with a group of evidently intellectual friends (discussing Karl Marx) but looks away from them to direct her attention to the more fun-loving girls who are talking about parties and suchlike and who form a clique that she obviously feels excluded from. Likewise, at college, the professor Janet has a crush on offers himself up to the class as an object of voyeuristic delight (he shows off his new socks and then repines seductively on his desk), and Janet can only look on with quivering, maddening desire (whereas the other students clearly know how to negotiate games of looking and power with a young professor).

At the same time, Janet is also someone that other people look at with a goal to dictating how she should be, how she should look, how she should act. This is a form of looking different from Janet's: in most cases, when she peers in on a reality, she engages in no intervention upon it and exhibits little ability to alter it (she is an observer, the quintessence of a writer's mode in the world), whereas the people around her endlessly look at her in order to mould her to their will. Obviously, the extreme example is the harsh treatment Janet receives in the asylum where each thing she does is observed, catalogued, controlled (she cannot even go to the bathroom without a nurse and other patients observing her). Throughout much of the film, Janet is submitted to the scrutiny of an official apparatus of powerful control: from school officials to medical officers to the family itself as an organ of rule-making and discipline (for instance, her stay during college at her aunt's house where she feels impelled to hide her periods and to eat furtively when her aunt is out of the room).

But even more benevolent attempts to intervene on her behalf are fraught with problematic consequences. For example, when Janet prepares to meet her English publisher, the woman she is boarding with is insistent on her coming up with a better hairstyle for herself (the results of which, as we see, are disastrous). Significantly, while some people look upon Janet with well-intentioned benevolence, their benevolent look is rarely an expression of envy along the lines of her own envious look back at them and others. That is, they have little jealousy of Janet, little desire to emulate her, and more often want to fashion her to their own ends. It might be noted that the most obvious situations in which others evince some envy of Janet – generally, a rare occurrence – happen once Janet has concretised her commitment to the writing career. For instance, the older writer Frank is obviously miffed that Janet has achieved the immediate success that eluded him, and a group of London intellectuals seem quite impressed that she has had books published (although one of the group redirects the conversation his way by suggesting that the publishing house he hopes to publish with – Faber & Faber – matters more than the local presses that brought out

Janet's books). For the most part, Janet has to learn to exist other than as an object of desire or envy for others, since that is rarely how others see her.

We might contrast this with the image of Ada in *The Piano* who gains strength by the captivation she holds over others, in the ways she makes them into desiring voyeurs. Ironically, whereas *The Piano* has been, as I noted earlier, the object of some celebration as a film that ostensibly realises Laura Mulvey's call for a woman's cinema that revises traditional patterns of filmic pleasure – insofar as the film reveals the helplessness in men's voyeurism – it would be as possible to posit *An Angel at My Table* as a 'Mulveyan' work. Where *The Piano* reinvigorates lush romanticism to make the female protagonist powerful, *An Angel at My Table* has its woman remove herself from the realm of glamorous seduction and avoids depicting her in romantic fashion. It is rare for Janet to be an object of voyeuristic delight either for characters in the film or for the spectator.

For instance, if the sex scenes in *The Piano* were applauded by some viewers for seeming to give the woman erotic force and making the male body an object of 'to-be-looked-at-ness', *An Angel at My Table* divests its one sex scene of eroticism. The scene's potential eroticism is undercut by the sheer narcissism of Bernard (interrupting foreplay to check out his lines of poetry), by Janet's evident timidity in entering into this new adventure and by the sheer evanescence the scene has in the overall course of the film. Certainly, there is display of the sexualised woman's body in the next scene as Janet swims nude in the shiny water of the Mediterranean and Bernard looks down admiringly at her. But this too is a fleeting moment, and the spectator's potential voyeurism bumps up against Bernard's and all the creepy self-centredness he represents. Soon, in fact, erotic display is something Janet will come to regret (and in the next scene, her Spanish neighbours judge her harshly for her sexual improprieties), a misguided romanticism that must be expunged by refusing to talk to Bernard and by aborting her pregnancy. In its sobriety toward sexuality, *An Angel at My Table* could be taken as a film that downplays 'visual pleasure'.

As she emerges from illness (and the early mis-diagnosis of it as schizophrenia), one of Janet's doctors tells her that she should avoid submission to the 'shoulds' of other people, the internalisation of their will and desire as her own. Janet has indeed to learn to live for herself, and this means both rethinking how she looks at the world and how she accepts its look back at her. She needs to give up envious voyeurism and to no longer care about the intentions of others. If *The Piano* presents a woman learning to grow by transferring her affection from an instrument of art to other people, *An Angel at My Table* offers an alternate feminine narrative, one about self-sufficiency, one about art as a salvation from the ravages of the social. Janet can still look out at the world but she now does so for the needs of her own imagination. Thus, in the last section, Janet looks out longingly at the richly blue ocean from her apartment window in Spain but she does so from a position of artistic control, from a recognition of the transformative potentials of the aesthetic dimension. Revealingly, the very next scene has Janet coping terribly with a social encounter as if to contrast her success in the private realm of imagination with her inability to be effective in an interpersonal one.

A modest art film with an avoidance of the pleasures of romantic cinema, *An Angel at My Table* had a success generally limited to art-cinema venues. It was, for instance, the first New Zealand film ever to be shown at the Venice Film Festival, and there it won the Silver Lion and Grand Jury prizes. In a nice irony – given debates about Campion's national identity (New Zealander? Australian?) – the Australian Film Critics' Circle awarded *An Angel at My Table* its prize for Best Foreign Film.

Five
After-Shocks

The Portrait of a Lady (1996)

A 1994 interview in the Australian press found Jane Campion at work on a new project at the moment that *The Piano*'s Oscar nominations came out:

> At the time, the New Zealand-born film-maker was holed up in a bungalow at the exclusive Kim's resort, a lush getaway on the Central Coast [of Australia] with writer/producer Billy MacKinnon and US producer Laurie Parker. They were working on the film adaptation of the Christopher Isherwood novel, *My Guru* [*and his disciple*] – one of Campion's upcoming projects.[1]

Writer Philip Lopate also seems to have worked on the adaptation at an earlier stage. But the Isherwood project was dropped. In fact, earlier interviews had Campion working on both *My Guru* and *The Portrait of a Lady* with a hesitation as to which should be started on first but with a plan to do both films at some point. In a mid-1993 interview, she has already announced that *The Portrait of a Lady* will come first and will go into production by November of that year.[2] Even if *My Guru* (about Isherwood's relationship in Hollywood with his guru) was not made, the Eastern motif of religious cult would be picked up in *Holy Smoke* which Campion decided to make after a trip to India.

One can only imagine that Jane Campion would have developed her projects after *The Piano* with both excitement and trepidation. On the one hand, the success of *The Piano* undoubtedly gave her a stronger basis to negotiate from and to recruit film-making resources for. On the other hand, *The Piano* certainly set high standards and expectations that Campion's subsequent productions would be judged against.

For the screenplay of *The Portrait of a Lady*, Campion went back to her *An Angel at My Table* writer, Laura Jones. A recurrent rumour has it that the film was pressed into production to beat a planned Merchant–Ivory adaptation of Henry James's novel. In an unpublished interview, however, James Ivory offers a more benign account. He and Campion both had the same agent in the USA and discovered that they were both working on adaptations of the James novel. It was decided that he should put aside his effort and he turned to another James novel.

Campion's film certainly doesn't seem to have had a rushed preparation. With a decision to do on-location shooting in a variety of European locales (for example, Salisbury, Rome, Florence), the film had a relatively long production history (there was a two-and-a-half-month shoot, a fact emphasised in the documentary on the film, *Portrait: Jane Campion and The Portrait of a Lady*, which introduces each segment of the production with a title indicating what week of the shoot they're in). Nicole Kidman, whom Campion evidently wanted to use as early as *A Girl's Own Story* (but who was then unavailable) played Isabel Archer. The first choice for the role of Gilbert Osmond was William Hurt but according to Campion, 'it bothered him to play an evil character with no redeeming features'.[3]

For Jones, the challenge was, as she put it, to 'go from six hundred and something pages of highly detailed narrative with its great, subtle, bold dialogue and structure ... to a screenplay of about 120 sparsely laid-out pages'.[4] As is typical of literary adaptation, the screenplay offers both a subtraction of elements from the novel and additions, some of which might be seen as attempts either to find visual substitutes for verbal subtleties or to engage in active transformation of the literary text into a filmic work that signals its own irreducible identity and difference from the original. The

An open ending

subtractions start with the first moment of the film's narrative: opening with Isabel turning down a marriage proposal from Lord Warburton, the film skips over the first eleven chapters. Gone, then, are the chronicle of Isabel's early life (her dissolute father, her retreat into a world of intellectuality combined with a curiosity desirous of learning about the world); the narrator commentaries (both positive and reserved) that set up her independence of character; the description of her uncle as a self-made American living in England, but taking a distance from its way of life (the film in fact makes Mr Touchett an Englishman, played by the eminent John Gielgud); the presentation of her aunt also as a strong-willed figure who lives her own life without compromise. Also subtracted from the course of the film are details of secondary stories of romance (for example, Henrietta Stackpole's growing love for Mr Bantling, Edward Rosier's background and his earlier acquaintance with Isabel).

And if the beginning of the film's narrative eliminates a great deal of preparatory material (what film students and film-industry types refer to as 'back story'), the ending also involves a subtraction of events. In an interview at the opening of her film at the Venice Film Festival, Campion put it this way, 'I'm too much of an optimist to really like the way James completes the novel.'[5] James's ending is famous (and, for some, notorious) for simul-

Buñuelian talking beans

taneously offering a momentous last decisive action (Isabel chooses to reject Goodwood's advances – at least for the present – and returns to Italy) and nonetheless shrouding the conclusion in ambiguity and openness: is she going back to assume her marriage with Osmond, is she planning to confront him and assert her independence?

Interestingly, Jones's original screenplay actually made explicit yet another possible outcome of Isabel's return to Italy as mentioned in the novel: her rescue of Pansy from the dismal and constrained life her father has designed for her. In Jones's screenplay, the very ending has Isabel coming to Pansy in the convent her father has consigned her to and offering her hand to pull Pansy out of the shadow (earlier, when Isabel had visited Pansy before going to England, Pansy had refused to go out into the light because her father had forbidden her to go beyond a specific limit on the property). To be sure, there is still ambiguity here – Pansy could refuse the solace being held out to her by Isabel – but the Jones ending still suggests a decisiveness to Isabel's final action that is never explicit in the novel. There are some indications that this ending was shot and then, when Campion felt dissatisfied, dropped. Instead, the film ends just after Isabel is kissed by Goodwood and rushes back to her aunt's house. Without the subsequent action of her returning to Italy, the film becomes even more open-ended perhaps than the novel: will Isabel remain in England? will she become receptive to Goodwood's overtures? will she return to Italy and either confront Osmond, or reconcile to her life with him, or rescue Pansy?

In addition to these subtractions, a number of the additions/substitutions have been the object of much critical attention. For example, when Isabel, after her first encounters with Osmond, leaves for a grand journey around Europe and the Middle East to try to find herself, we are offered a black-and-white sequence deliberately referencing several forms of early cinema: silent comedy (a jerky camera that catches the staccato gestures of Isabel and Henrietta on the bow of a ship); an exotic film *à la The Sheik* of a journey to the 'Orient'; Buñuelian surrealism as beans on Isabel's plate with flies buzzing above them begin to talk and repeat Osmond's declaration that he is absolutely in love with Isabel.

The most discussed addition to the film comes at the very beginning. If the first *narrative* moment signals the elimination of a long stretch of the novel, this abrupt entrance into the narrative is, in fact, preceded by a non-narrative prologue, initially of sound alone and then of image alone. In this prologue, shot in a crisp black and white, with a few instances of colour, we first hear women talking of romance (for example, what it means to be kissed) and then we see modern women (some with Sony Walkmans) in the woods, dancing, posing, touching, looking enigmatically at the camera (see colour section, between pp.90–1). In the words of the screenplay, they are 'Independent, impatient, unacquainted with pain, a confidence at once innocent and dogmatic, spontaneous, full of theories, with delicate, desultory, flamelike spirits, facing their destinies'.[6]

For the most part, critics disliked this opening, although it did have a few defenders. One approving commentator, William E. Shriver, argues that the prologue bears on the rest of the film by providing a context to understand narrative developments in Isabel's world. Specifically, against the common charge by critics that the film doesn't motivate Isabel's captivation by Osmond to sufficiently credible degree, Shriver asserts that Isabel is, in fact, not so much seduced by Osmond as pushed towards him by a world of women as the really decisive community behind a woman's choices: in Shriver's words,

> In my opinion, it was not necessary for us to see why Isabel fell for Osmond. Recall the pre-title sequence, which seemed to promise a story where the linkage of woman-to-woman would be more significant than that of woman-to-man. Campion met her obligation to explain the transition preceding Isabel's marriage to Osmond by showing – most vividly – Isabel 'falling for' for the two women who would bind her to Osmond: Madame Merle, who, for her own purposes, put Isabel 'in [Osmond's] way'; and Pansy, Osmond's daughter, at whose service Isabel will place all her strength.[7]

Interestingly, this reading has the effect of modifying the feel-good New Agey feminine community image of the prologue to render the relations between women as possibly less innocent and supportive; this would be in keeping with a recurrent emphasis in Campion's films on the potential conflictual nature of women's relations. But this is a reading that very few

'A kiss like white lightning, a flash'

commentators adopted; instead, they tended to take the opening as an unselfconscious depiction of the Community of Women.

As several commentators have pointed out, it is notable that the very first thing we hear the women speaking about in the prologue is specifically the romantic nature of kissing, since another addition/substitution the film makes is to emphasise erotically charged kisses between men and women. To be sure, the novel moves toward the energetic and disturbing kiss that Caspar Goodwood gives Isabel, described in the very last pages of the novel as a kiss 'like white lightning, a flash that spread and spread again, and stayed'. But the film makes literal the erotic charge that seems to underlie numerous relationships in the novel and that generally remains implicit there. For example, Gilbert Osmond gives Isabel a deep kiss when he comes upon her in Ravenna and this fuels her obsession for him (as one critic of the film says, 'Basically, Campion's *Portrait of a Lady* boils down to the story of a girl who married the wrong man because his kiss featured a good deal more tongue than any Victorian girl had reason to expect').[8] Likewise, when Isabel goes to the dying Ralph Touchett and admits that he was the one she (should have) loved all along, she lies next to him on his deathbed and showers him with kisses. Significantly, while Laura Jones speaks in her preface to the film's screenplay of two primary secrets in the novel – the plot that Madame Merle undertakes with Gilbert Osmond to have him marry Isabel and win her fortune, the revelation that Madame Merle was Osmond's lover and the mother of his child (I would add a third secret at least to the novel's intent: namely, Ralph conspiring with his father to have a fortune left to Isabel) – the rendering literal of erotic connection through the representation of a kiss has somewhat the effect of altering the impact of the second secret's revelation. That there is something sexual between Osmond and Madame Merle is made clear from the start.

Perhaps the most striking – and for many critics, the most controversial – addition of kissing in the film comes in an imaginary sequence: just after rejecting Goodwood's offer of marriage and having already turned down Lord Warburton, Isabel, alone in her room, begins to swoon with erotic delight, caressing her forehead with the tassels over her canopy-bed and then as she sinks onto the bed we see Warburton and Goodwood languorously kissing her all over while Ralph Touchett looks on.

But for all its attempt to literalise the eroticism implicit in the novel's relationships, *Portrait* was taken by many commentators to be a cold, unerotic work. A period piece like *The Piano*, *Portrait* uses its historical moment to speak of a society of constraint, and this is played out in the imposing, even enveloping, nature of buildings; in the binding of characters to rules and procedures of social propriety; in the enclosure of people in costumes that regulate and stifle. For example, the props of the Victorian moment are shown to be implements of constraint most explicitly in a ballroom sequence where young women, tied up tight in their gowns, are fainting from their bodily confinement.

And in this society of constraint, Isabel, like many other Campion women, takes up a somewhat masochistic position – a fantasy of surrendering to a seductive and potentially dangerous man. Thus when Ralph Touchett tries to dissuade her from marrying Osmond by declaring that in such a union she will be 'caught' and put 'in a cage', Isabel replies, 'If I like my cage, that needn't trouble you', and the point is echoed by the composition which frames Isabel against bars that resemble nothing so much as a cage.

Visually, *The Portrait of a Lady* establishes an air of enclosure first by being

Caged

very much a film of interiors, of literally bound environments. It is perhaps appropriate that Campion evidently at one point thought of doing *Portrait* as a theatre piece (and that one tryout of the script was done evidently as a stage reading). For a period piece shot on location, it contains a majority of scenes shot indoors, in spaces filled with imposing objects of collection (the bibelots that are referred to at several points in the film). Indeed, one consequence of the film's dropping of the first eleven chapters is that the novel's sunny opening – the Touchett men and Lord Warburton enjoying tea on the lawn at Gardencourt overlooking a river – is minimised, being transformed into no more than a meagre glimpse of a tea party that Isabel rushes past and disrupts. With this transformation of the lawn scene into a mere fleeting impression, a world of buoyant openness disappears. Instead, starting on a tight close-up of Isabel among the tangles of a nature that can seem as much to entrap her as to offer open possibility, the film remains in a fairly claustrophic space that bespeaks confinement and restraint. A review by Australian film scholar Brian McFarlane captures the way the dour look of the film fits its theme of entrapment and the closing off of options for an adventurous being (see colour section, between pp.90–1). McFarlane notes how there is 'a sudden burst of brilliant light when the scene shifts to Florence' but suggests that the film offers this luminosity only so that it can then shut it down:

> Campion moves us quickly indoors to show Madame Merle at work tempting Osmond to make a play for Isabel. Isabel is often glimpsed briefly as light in dark places, but there is little sense of light after she marries Osmond and her openness to life becomes constrained. ... The darkening of the drama is created in this control [of the *mise-en-scène*]: the film's colour range seems to be mainly a matter of browns and blues, and the often-claustrophobic insistence on interiors makes its own point about the nature of the film's interests.[9]

The film's insistence on an oppressive and deadening environment is so strong that, for some critics, those stylistic flourishes that might interject momentary glimpses of escape from a controlling order are read instead as ineffective, powerless. In particular, several critics note that in several instances the film composes isolated shots at a tilt, implying perhaps an attempt at overthrowing the imperious weight of the dominant order. Thus, in the opening sequence – where Isabel refuses Lord Warburton's offer and strides back into the house past the tea party – the segment devoted to the party begins with a fairly symmetrical shot of Warburton's two sisters in extreme foreground talking about Isabel as she emerges from the garden, a small figure framed by the two women. This tightly balanced composition, which might be taken to indicate Isabel's fixation in a social order that is weaving its plans for her, is answered a few shots later by off-kilter images of Isabel striding past the tea party and then in a dramatic overhead shot sweeping up a dog that's been following her and who she plays with by growling at him. The composition and the vibrant energy of Isabel's actions would seem to indicate the force of a free spirit who fights against order and restriction.

But the tilted shot in general is one that calls attention to itself, one that directly speaks of the intention to produce a marked effect (that is, someone had quite consciously to decide to tilt the camera). The tilt can easily have something artificial about it, and the relative paucity of such shots in the course of the film can give them little force against the film's general sense of well-disciplined control. Moreover, the very fact that the canting of the image as Isabel sweeps past the tea party occurs quickly and at the very beginning of the film gives it little force in the face of a narrative that

From symmetry to the off-kilter

will so overwhelmingly chronicle the confinement and exploitation of Isabel. Where stylistic deviations from the norm were systematic in early films like *Sweetie*, their use in *The Portrait of a Lady* is sporadic. Moreover, the rarity of tilted compositions means that when they do pop up, they can seem, as many critics indicated, all the more forced rather than forceful. Thus, when the film shifts to Italy, one sequence begins with a palace shot at an extremely tilted angle that then straightens itself. Like the black-and-white travelogue sequence that bothered many viewers, such evident manipulations of the film image as offered up by the tilt were taken by many critics of *The Portrait of a Lady* as signalling a mechanical attempt to infuse flourish into a film that is generally about the stifling of flourish.

For the most part, space in *The Portrait of a Lady* is solidly in place and imposes its weightiness on its inhabitants. But as with a theatrical chamber-piece, what really presses in on individuals is less space itself than the other people who come to take up position within it (the hell that is 'other people', in Jean-Paul Sartre's aptly titled *Huis clos* [*No Exit*]). Within its geographies of the interior, the film images people and their socially circumscribed interactions in ways that reiterate the claustrophobic tone. In particular, the film is filled with very tight shots of faces without much space beyond them. Interestingly, although cinematographer Stuart Dryburgh shot the film in widescreen format, the composition rarely invokes the clash-filled staging of earlier Campion films, a staging in which a face in the extreme foreground is balanced against figures in the background of the frame. *The Portrait of a Lady* does not play with contrasts of scale from front to back in the image. Instead, the area of the frame around the faces in close-up in *The Portrait of a Lady* is emptied out by ink-dark shadows. To be sure, there are intense pools of light in the film (most strikingly in the sequence in the catacombs where light streams down into the underground space where Isabel and Osmond circle seductively around each other), but as Dryburgh recounts, 'The light that floods the rooms is strong sunlight that falls off very fast. If someone was standing at the window, they were brightly illuminated (see colour section, between pp.90–1); if they were six feet away, they'd start to go into shadow; and if they were on the other side, we'd go into blackness photographically.'[10] Rather than always seeing this fall-off of luminosity as something to work against, the film-makers use the obscuring of light to emphasise a tightly closed world for the characters who inhabit it. And this sense of a world thrown into claustrophobic obscurity even infiltrates the film's manner of photographing the characters themselves. In particular, the face of the characters becomes a site for calculated plays of the contrast of light and dark. As Dryburgh explains,

> What I would try to do – and this is where I would try to influence the blocking, not always successfully – is to keep the light on the dark side of the room, more behind the actors. Essentially, the side of their faces that was more toward the camera would remain dark. But they would be defined by backlight or three-quarter backlight from the windows. Sometimes we'd even silhouette them against the windows. We were really pursuing the edge of darkness there.
>
> I don't relish making the comparison, but my approach was inspired by Dutch masters like Rembrandt or Vermeer – the way they would use natural light, with subjects and delineations and objects at the far end of the source decreasingly exposed. We actually looked at quite a few examples of that sort of art for the quality of the light.[11]

A good example of this filming of characters themselves as caught up in the obscurity of space occurs early in the film when Isabel has returned to Gardencourt where her uncle has been taken ill. The previous sequence ends with a close-up of an insect trapped inside a glass, an insistent image of the film's narrative of entrapment. From this, we cut to a shot of the exterior of Gardencourt caught in a dreary downpour and framed between the symmetrical rectangles of hedges on either side of the frame, an image again of a stifling world with little spontaneity in it. This is followed by a shot of Isabel at a window, filmed with the camera inside shooting past her toward the outside and turning her fully into a silhouette with other silhouetted figures (the domestic staff) passing before her as so many blurry and darkened shapes. We might contrast this hopeless image of a woman waiting by a window in the rain with the one of Ada in *The Piano* that I discussed much earlier. Where Ada tears away from the wedding photo session to look out of the window and be connected by imagination to her faraway piano, Isabel is turned away from the window to participate in party preparations that obviously she has little enthusiasm for but that her social role requires her to engage in.

Swaddled in the tight clothes of her class, Isabel wends her way through an environment that is stifling, weighty, oppressive in its dark overbearing inevitability. The falling off of light around the characters that Dryburgh speaks of is complemented in several shots by a slow motion that lessens

Isabel's pace and makes it seem as if she is struggling her way through a thick, gaseous surround. And as Dryburgh explains, this concentration on characters in their constrained intimacy was further emphasised by a deliberate blurring of the focus on the background. Dryburgh shot the film primarily using long lenses with consequences that he explains:

> A lot of the movie was shot at very long lengths – 100 mm, 200 mm – which tends to isolate the characters and put the background out of focus. You're only seeing a very small portion of the background, maybe a six-foot square. It becomes sort of a medley of color, texture, light and shade. The emphasis is on the characters rather than on what's behind or around them.[12]

Dryburgh goes on to talk of another stylistic quality of the film, its omnipresent sense of motion. As the article on his work on the film in *American Cinematographer* explains,

> The camera is in a state of constant motion throughout the film, as virtually every shot was executed on a dolly. Ironically, there is no sense of 'portrait photography' in the illustrative sense. Likewise, there are no conventional master shots with encroaching coverage [i.e. there are no overall long shots of a scene that would establish the place of people in the setting and that could then give way to closer views of details in the scene], but rather choreographed camera moves that indirectly establish a sense of the environment.[13]

As Dryburgh himself elaborates, '[W]e ... kept the camera moving in order to maintain a sort of emotional restlessness and a sense of not being quite sure of what is going on.'[14] This reference to restlessness and confusion is important as it suggests a use of motion not to imply freedom and possibility but to add to the dilemmas of entrapment that the film chronicles. Movement in *The Portrait of a Lady* does not so much hint at an exhilarating liberatory potential – such as we might see, for instance, in the Hollywood musical where camera movement in song-and-dance sequences can offer an image of a space opened up to human possibility or as we saw with the lush romantic camera movements of the romantic tradition that *The Piano* derives from – so much as it offers another degree of enclosure for its characters. Generally, there are three sorts of movement in the film. There is the movement of characters through corridors or object-filled rooms (or in a few cases, through paths in carefully laid-out gardens). Characters advance, but according to limits imposed by the very space that houses them. They are like the insect – trapped in a glass and able to do little more than beat its wings feverishly against the conditions of its imprisonment. A second form of movement in the film involves characters circling around one another as if sizing up an opponent or staking out a prey. For example, in the scene of seduction between Isabel and Osmond in the catacombs, the two potential lovers glide tactically about each other, turning romance into a ballet made up of feints and forays. Third, there is the movement that Dryburgh is talking about – the weaving of the camera around characters, a choreography between people and the manner of filming them. These three forms of movement can work separately or concurrently to structure personal trajectory – Isabel's especially – as circumscribed, as able to move forward only under the shadow of preset options.

We might suggest that in its rendition of a woman who becomes captivated by a mysterious stranger, *The Portrait of a Lady* modifies in particularly pessimistic directions the dynamic of the Gothic film as I outlined it earlier. In the works of this genre tradition, as we've seen, a woman finds ways to move from a dangerous relationship to one filled with sympathy and sensitivity (whether by finding these qualities in the originally rough male figure or by finding an alternative to the husband that the woman can transfer affection to). But in *The Portrait of a Lady*, Isabel turns to the dangerous Gilbert Osmond *after* knowing, and rejecting, more sensitive suitors (the sickly Ralph Touchett, the overly refined Lord Warburton, the pragmatically uninspiring Caspar Goodwood). That is, by the time Isabel meets Osmond, she has already evaluated the offerings of a more caring male world and rejected it. The film cannot subsequently hold out this sensitive, empathetic world as a positive alternative, especially because the social constraints of her position and a perhaps misplaced pride mean that Isabel cannot for a long time show to others that she knows she made a mistake in marrying Osmond. There is no going back. Where the traditional form of the Gothic film represents marriage with a mysterious stranger as the first step in a process of growth, *The Portrait of a Lady* offers such a marriage as the end of a trajectory, and this sets up the narrative as a dramatisation of perdition.

Obviously, this theme of failed union as the endpoint of a young woman's quest is already present in the James novel but it could easily be argued that even more than in the literary work, the film strips Isabel of much of her will and of much of her ability to fight back effectively against the systems of constraint. Take, for instance, the difference in the way the novel and the film represent a conversation that Isabel has with her aunt about Isabel's desire to make choices for herself. At the end of the seventh chapter in the novel, Isabel is told by her aunt that it is improper for a young lady to stay up with two men (Ralph Touchett and Lord Warburton) without a female chaperone. The following conversation ensues, terminating with Isabel's buoyant declaration of independence:

> 'Of course, you're vexed at my interfering with you,' said Mrs Touchett.
> Isabel considered. 'I'm not vexed, but I'm surprised – and a good deal mystified. Wasn't it proper I should remain in the drawing room?'
> 'Not in the least. Young girls here – in decent houses – don't sit alone with the gentlemen late at night.'
> 'You were right to tell me then,' said Isabel. 'I don't understand it, but I'm very glad to know it.'
> 'I shall always tell you,' her aunt answered, 'whenever I see you taking what seems to me too much liberty.'
> 'Pray do: but I don't say I shall always think your remonstrances just.'
> 'Very likely not. You're too fond of your own ways.'
> 'Yes, I think I'm very fond of them. But I always want to know the things one shouldn't do.'
> 'So as to do them?' asked her aunt.
> 'So as to choose,' said Isabel.[15]

In the film, the comparable exchange takes place as Isabel prepares to go to London to meet Henrietta and her aunt comments on the improprieties of her thinking about going alone. The dialogue incorporates some phrases from the chronologically earlier interchange in the novel, but it leaves out the forcefulness of Isabel's resistance. Here is the script's rendition of the interchange:

> Mrs Touchett: Your uncle is right – you certainly can't go to London without an escort …
>
> Isabel: Isn't anything proper here?
>
> Mrs Touchett: You're too fond of your own ways. [Interestingly, the film version adds the word, 'Missy', emphasising even more, like an admonishment, Mrs Touchett's intent to place Isabel in a position of obedience.]
>
> Isabel: Yes, I'm very fond of them.
>
> Mrs Touchett: I don't expect you to heed my advice, but as you have neither mother nor father, I do expect you to listen to it.[16]

To be sure, there is in Mrs Touchett's last phrase the admission that Isabel might nonetheless go her own way, but Isabel is still being instructed in and into the limits of a way of life (and Shelley Winters's tough and forceful delivery of the lines makes their import as commands all the more authoritative and unchallengeable). There is much less expression here of Isabel's self-determination and will to be free.

The Piano had implied that in the antipodes of the colonialist project a life lived at the edges of the dominant culture could have the potential for change, for moving to new forms of relationship not based on commerce and possessiveness. Likewise, *Holy Smoke* would suggest that in the frontier space of the Australian desert, there might also be the possibility for breaking from the constraints of one's origins. In contrast, *The Portrait of a Lady* fully takes place within the geography of the dominant order and offers little space in which one can break out in new directions. But for the scenes in which Isabel goes on her grand tour – scenes in which her distance from indigenous peoples is suggested by her dismay and by a rear projection that literally separates her off from other cultures – and for a few shots of domestic staff and anonymous passers-by in the film's few shots of public places, *The Portrait of a Lady* moves in a world of Western privilege where little glimpse of alternate experience or of other life options is visible. This world of privilege is represented as one particularly enclosed upon itself and caught up in the restrictions of highly elaborated social codes for what one has to do and what one has to be. More than Campion's other films, *The Portrait of a Lady* is obsessed by entrapment and enclosure. We might note, for instance, how the motif of

Class privilege against the backdrop of a distant world

capture and possession runs through the film. Significantly, a number of the figures in the milieu of the film are collectors, and there is the sense of a world driven by ownership, by control (even the kindly Ralph Touchett is shown trapping the insect in a cup, a direct image of capture).

In one classic film of the Gothic romantic tradition, Vincente Minnelli's adaptation of Flaubert's *Madame Bovary*, there is an exuberant scene when, at a ball, Emma Bovary begins to feel faint in the swirl of a vibrant dance and orders are given to the servants to smash the ballroom's windows to allow in more air; as Emma and her partner swoop and pirouette energetically, there is intercut a frenetic montage of glass being shattered violently. We might contrast the exhilarating frenzy of this sequence, with its demonstration to Emma of the potentials of a high-society life, with the scene I've already cited in *The Portrait of a Lady* in which young ladies faint from their corseting during a society ball. But for a few moments – Isabel's self-willed rush past the tea party at the film's very beginning, her passionate fantasy of being loved by three men, among others – there is little sense in *The Portrait of a Lady* of vital possibility, of energetic self-expression and a passionate swelling up of desire and determination. *The Portrait of a Lady* is in many ways a cold, even despairing, work.

Whether the lifelessness of the film was deliberate or not – and I have suggested some of the ways in which the film *systematically* depicts in both story and style a world given over to the stifling of emotions and energies – the film met with criticism. Many critics disliked its bleakness and coldness; disliked what they saw as its lifeless and mechanical acting (John Malkovich as Gilbert Osmond came in for especial condemnation; it should be noted though that there was consistent praise for Barbara Hershey); disliked it for its disruptions of its narrative world with modern interpolations or fantasy sequences (the scene of lovemaking with the three men, the silent movie version of Isabel's tourism and especially the prologue of women communing in the woods which met with general dislike). Although she wrote favourably about *The Portrait of a Lady*, film critic Kathleen Murphy's description of the film's downbeat narrative of stifling confinement well captures the tone of the film, a tone that inevitably would disappoint many spectators after *The Piano*:

> The austere classicism of *Portrait*, perfectly expressing Henry James's epistemological/moral scrupulousness, lent Campion's masterpiece the kind of searing force from which fans of sentimentalised Austen and sexualised James could only shy away. Campion imagined Gilbert Osmond, Isabel's nemesis, as a Luciferian 'director' who seduces his wide-eyed angle into a poisoned *mise-en-scène* where he sadistically diminishes and darkens everything and everyone. Think of all Campion's virgins – girlfriends, sisters, writer, pianist, artist of the beautiful – as bright flames that flicker between creativity and nihilism, innocence and madness, epiphany and 'the big, black nothing.'[17]

The Portrait of a Lady is, in its own way, a film that avoids 'visual pleasure'. In contrast, as we've seen, *The Piano* was taken by many of its fans to matter precisely because it offered intensities of pleasure, because its visual style was inspiring, because its subject matter tapped into erotic fantasy (this despite the violence of the film). Whether viewed as a success or a failure, *The Portrait of a Lady* could only be taken as a harsh break from the elaboration of a vibrant romantic cinema. It is a film that refuses resolutely to represent an easy image of female empowerment as demanded by the conventions of a certain kind of woman's film.

Holy Smoke (1999)

After *Portrait of a Lady*, spectators and the critical establishment generally greeted Campion's next effort, *Holy Smoke*, as a whimsical work, a return to the 'quirky' universe of the early films with their trenchant satire of the foibles of everyday life. Even reviewers who liked the film tended to take its own modesty as a cause for gentle appraisal and offered little more than modest praise. And for those who disliked the film, it seemed to confirm that *The Piano* had been a fluke, the subsequent work signalling a decline in quality.[18]

According to a notice in the *New York Times*, Jane Campion reportedly came up with the idea for *Holy Smoke* in mid-air on a return to Sydney from a trip to India. Her subsequent comments in that piece might make the film seem the affirmative outcome of a spiritual quest:

> I wanted to make a contemporary film and just explore the subject of spirituality and the confusion about it. I've been to India. I've never joined an ashram or anything like that. But I kept thinking for years that I wanted to try to make some sense of what you think your purpose is. Is there a way of living that makes better sense?[19]

Certainly, however, on the basis of the critical response to the film, it is quite possible to feel that *Holy Smoke* in no evident, easy or inevitable way offers its viewers the means to judge whether or not this or that 'way of living ... makes better sense' and is rarely taken by them even to be raising this question. In a revealing parallel, both Ruth and her mother are asked at different points in the film about what they take the ultimate purpose of a human life to be, and both wonder at first if this is a trick or fake question: Ruth's commitment to the spiritual life is no more thought-out, no more secure, no more profound, than her mother's own hesitant engagement with the world around her. For many viewers, *Holy Smoke* is only minimally a serious investigation of spiritual quest; indeed, many critics of the film focused on the ways the film quickly leaves its Indian origin to become a battle of the sexes. (In an interview, Campion attributes some of the ambiguity in the film's image of spirituality to the collaboration with her sister on the screenplay: 'She's quite agnostic. I didn't realise to what extent. She

Wisps

hadn't thought about anything at all either and I'd be getting quite frustrated with her and at the same time it was really good because it was helpful to me to have a partner who had completely different beliefs.'[20]

The opening credits for *Holy Smoke* figure the film's title as light wisps of vapour that coalesce into letters. We might take this way of introducing the film as an apt image for the whole of *Holy Smoke*. First, the ethereal quality of these words formed from wafting steam signals a lightness, even an insubstantiality, that characterises the film. After the deep emotionalism of *The Piano* and the intellectual coldness of *The Portrait of a Lady*, *Holy Smoke* is permeated by an unpretentiousness. For instance, although it stars big names (for example, Kate Winslet soon after her success in *Titanic*) and although it sports numerous shots of vistas of the Australian outback, there's an unassuming smallness to the film.

In fact, the film often adopts a lightness of tone toward its modest narrative. At several points in *Holy Smoke*, for example, a seemingly serious action or attitude of a character is undercut by a whimsical flourish in cinematic style: to cite just one case, when Ruth affirms to P. J. that she has had serious relationships in the past, there is a cut to kitschy images overladen with tacky music of somewhat goofy-looking young guys who seem anything but serious. Even in its primary advertising campaign, *Holy Smoke* signalled

Remnants of quirky style

Modest and conventional style

its comic, deflating approach: the image used in newspaper ads and on posters mimics the cover of a tabloid magazine and announces itself as a 'Sizzling Late Edition' with the caption 'Sex captive in desert hideaway – young beauty seduced by macho American twice her age', ending with the question 'Has writer-director Jane Campion gone too far?' Obviously, after the gravity of *The Portrait of a Lady*, there was a decision to market the new film as a wacky work that doesn't take itself too seriously.

The lack of pretension in the film – especially after it moves away from a concentration on spiritual quest – is matched by a modesty in style. In fact, but for its vistas and for a few scenes with kitschy special effects, *Holy Smoke* adopts a fairly conventional, expressively subdued look. While critics found it a return to the quirkiness of Campion's earliest endeavours, stylistically the film is perhaps closest in look to *An Angel at My Table* with its sobriety of cinematic technique. Certainly, there is, at times, setting up of distortion and striking contrast through depth staging and filming of a sort we find in *Sweetie* and the short films (for instance, when the family goes to pick up P. J. at the airport, several shots outside oddly include a wedding couple being photographed against the concrete of the roadway). But this quirky framing in depth tends to be reserved for those scenes of *Holy Smoke* that set out to mock the tackiness of suburban life (that of Ruth's family). Once P. J. and Ruth move to the outback house where the cult de-programming is supposed to take place, the film settles into a fairly unassuming classical style governed by cuts back and forth between the two figures as they spar verbally with one another. Many moments are dominated by a editing strategy, quite conventionalised in the history of film, in which one person is seen over the shoulder of another and then a reverse-shot sets up a similar composition in the reverse direction. This style contributes to the modesty of *Holy Smoke*. And in this, it contributes also to the film's centring in on a verbal battle of the sexes. Once Ruth and P. J. move away from the garishness of family and suburban influence, *Holy Smoke* becomes a virtual minimalist work where little happens except endless verbal interchange. The film becomes claustrophobic and even painful. Many of these scenes seem like theatrical chamber-pieces in which a tightly limited group of characters interact with each other in tight spaces and in which there is a relentlessness that challenges the spectator. At best, the sense of confinement (not only of characters but of a tight filmic style) is opened up a bit by a frequent use of a moving camera that glides around characters (especially when Ruth and P. J. move outside for several spats). But here too, the camera movement is rarely ostentatious. Rather, it is generally tied to a focus on a character centrally in the frame, and fits an emphasis on a battle of the sexes in which each character is endlessly jockeying for a new position of power by stealthily circling around the other as a sort of prey.

Additionally, the wispy puffs of vapour that morph into words can also seem a signal of the film's general concern with a mutability of positions, with a lack of fixity to identities and attitudes. In a journal she kept during the film's shooting, Anna Campion describes the Australian outback, where so much of the film's narrative transpires, as 'a continuous morphing with topography, plants, planets, animals, people'.[21] In the outback especially, the characters change and move through new positions (especially in relation to each other). At the same time, the film's desire to float through a series of positions is in keeping with its lightness of tone: no viewpoint is taken as final, no emotion or attitude is endorsed as having unambiguous moral possession of truth and rightness. The editing style of cutting back and forth between characters and the weaving of camera around characters sets up filmic space as one in which characters vie for domination but where the balance of power can be tipped back at any moment (by a simple cut, for instance). The mocking tone is extended to so many different perspectives in the film that it becomes a work of undecidability in which there is no easy way to determine just what the point is.

Take, for instance, the title sequence. Over shots of Ruth and other Europeans who have come to India for exoticism and salvation, there plays a song by Neil Diamond ('Holy Holy'), for many an epitome of a syrupy kitsch of 1970s pop culture (although it comes with a drive and earnest energy that can also be captivating, and many critics applauded the vitality of this opening). The music seems at first not to be coming from within the Indian world depicted but from a non-synchronous track that is commenting on the image, perhaps signalling the stereotypical nature of the quest by lost and searching Western youth for Eastern salvation. (We might even note that the recording seems to be of a concert performance since it begins with people applauding, further signalling the theatricalised and distanced nature of this musical offering.) But by the end of the sequence, we see both Westerners and Indians alike dancing in harmony with the sound, and it seems that the musical commentary has perhaps been part of the story's narrative universe all along.

Neil Diamond as the union of East and West

Significantly, the transition from music over the image to music in the image comes just after Ruth, with great curiosity on her face, sees a group of religious converts pass before her, followed by a cut to her in a courtyard swirling around and looking up towards the rooftop above her where young people are energetically dancing and mouthing the words to the song. While the first shots in this transition suggest Ruth's quest for religious meaning – for example, the searching look upwards – the fact that this rooftop pictured above the rest of the city offers not spiritual uplift but an

Touched by religion

immersion in cheesy American culture undercuts any clear-cut notion of religious quest. Is the goal of these young people to achieve spirituality or just to go to a good party? There is no automatic way to take this opening sequence. For one on-line critic on one website, 'There is no sense of kitsch in the use of the song and the gospel-like sounds infuse the images with a holy rolling jolt of giddy energy.'[22] In contrast, for another web reviewer, 'The opening ... is so awful it suggests self-parody. It's a compendium of all of Campion's worst impulses as a film-maker: dubious music (tourists dancing ecstatically to, of all things, Neil Diamond's "Holy Holy"), turgid pace, pointless slow motion shots so "artful" in their beauty that they stop the film dead in its tracks.'[23]

What indeed do we make of *Holy Smoke*'s use of kitsch imagery and association? In the film's satire of the supposed tastelessness, triviality and downright silliness of suburban lifestyle, it is easy to understand the recourse to campiness. And when P. J. is introduced by means of another Neil Diamond song ('I am ... I said'), the music here seems quite appropriately sardonic: P. J. bears all the kitsch markings of 1970s cheesy culture, including swaggering machismo. But moments of spirituality and vision are also treated in terms of a style that resonates with tackiness, and this contributes to the film's undecidability of tone.

Take, for instance, the early scene in which Ruth has her religious conversion in India: in radiantly garish lighting, with darting rays of light produced by chintzy special effects, Ruth is touched on the forehead by the guru Baba and swoons as op-art and pop-art images float around her like some sort of kitsch revival of psychedelic cinema (see colour section, between pp.90–1). In an interview, digital effects supervisor Andy Brown explains some of the creation of the look of *Holy Smoke* with specific reference to this scene: cinematographer 'Dion [Beebe] filmed the scene with the bold colours already in shot – gold, magenta, white. We enhanced the religious iconography by isolating these colours, ensuring sufficient contrast whilst softening off highlights.'[24] The scene comes off as unreal, but it is all too easy to take it less as the transcendental unreality of religious uplift than as a deliberately corny and cartoony rendition of the limited nature of religious ecstasy in an impressionable young woman.

The ambiguities of the sequence are further amplified by the fact that this scene of conversion is part of a flashback (Ruth's friend, Prue, has returned to Australia to tell Ruth's family what happened) and its corny look could be taken to dramatise either Prue's cynical attitude toward the unreality of this supposed religious experience or Ruth's own image of the events filtered through her obviously girlish and mass-culture-filled mind. Later, indeed, when Ruth's old Australian girlfriends come to see her on her return home, she reverts to chummy giggles and when she drives, dressed in a sari, out to visit her dad, she sings and dances to rock music. For all her conversion to 'Eastern' religion, Ruth remains very much a spoiled, white Westerner – this, indeed, is P. J.'s telling criticism of her later on, and we see its sting. It is easy to imagine that a young woman like Ruth would experience what she took to be religious experience in precisely the sappy, tacky way depicted in her 'conversion'. (Likewise, when towards the end of the film, P. J. has his own religious vision, this man of the 1970s sees a floating image of Ruth as an Indian goddess with many arms, filmed in kitsch style and undulating to the Burt Bacharach pop song 'Baby, It's You'.) It's hard, then, to know how to take the scene of Ruth's conversion, and that undecidability influences the reception of the rest of the film since it affects our understanding of the stakes of the battle of wits between Ruth and her family and between Ruth and P. J. over the ostensible profundity of her new-found devotion.

If *The Piano* and *The Portrait of a Lady* can appear, in optimistic and pessimistic fashion respectively, to derive from the Gothic tradition's emphasis on an oppressive confinement of femininity, *Holy Smoke* can easily be related to another genre, the screwball comedy. To be sure, the film is Gothic in its image of a woman's entrapment – for example, the painful sequence in which Ruth's family surround her in order to force her into cult de-programming – and even more specifically in an entrapment in a domestic space. In an isolated house far from civilisation (like, say, *Rebecca*'s Manderlay), Ruth tries to assert her will against a strong male foreigner who alternately seems to represent menace or sexual salvation.

Like the divided masculinity of the Gothic, P. J. embodies both redemption and villainy (he is the outsider figure from elsewhere who spirits the heroine off to her isolation). But where the Gothic male is exotic, P. J. is all

The frog who became king

too banal and readable: Ruth knows his type, knows how he has produced his look (one of her earliest barbs has to do with his dyed hair). Along with its satire of suburbia, *Holy Smoke* recognises a cheesiness in American popular culture and in that specific embodiment of that culture in anachronistic machismo. P. J. is introduced in the film with the markings both of the fairy-tale hero come to rescue the fair maiden and of an all-too prosaic figure of the modern age stuck in reactionary ideology and regressive personal style. On the one hand, the first images of P. J. – the camera sweeping upwards as he forcefully stands erect in foreground – present him as a veritable incarnation of fairy-tale heroism (the Neil Diamond song over this introduction refers to 'a frog who dreamed of being a king and then became one'). On the other hand, the scene is played as cliché with a recognition of P. J.'s macho tackiness (the sleazy look) and a comic deflation of machismo (P. J. uses his prowess only to free up some airport baggage trolleys and stare down a seemingly even more macho guy).

It is P. J.'s evident inadequacies as redemptive hero and unpreparedness for a modern battle of the sexes that means that his efforts to save and control Ruth, this film's 'fairy princess', are so easily resisted by her. Unlike the typical scenario for the woman in the Gothic space of the isolated house, Ruth very quickly re-establishes a balance of power that makes her

Screwball comedy for the 90s

more like the screwball heroine in her manipulations of the battles of sexuality.

It may be that the Gothic and the screwball comedy are variant (and often inverse) forms of a singular cultural representation of the modern battle of the sexes.[25] The screwball gains its affirmative qualities not only from an ending in which a heterosexual couple is formed in love (the ending, in fact, of so many Gothic narratives in which the heroine emerges into love from the darkness of menace) but also from moment-to-moment transfers of power from one sex to the other throughout the course of the narrative. The Gothic is about a woman's powerlessness – with her discovering power only at the very end (Isabel Archer beginning to stand up to her husband) or remaining in powerlessness and needing a man to save her (Ada saved by Baines and helped by him to discover her true power for love) – but the screwball comedy is more often about scene-to-scene shifts of power, momentary victories of both sexes in their continuing battle of love. Philosopher Stanley Cavell has referred to one tradition in the screwball film as 'the comedy of re-marriage', emphasising that this is a genre in which both the man and the woman have already known love and sexuality, have already grown into a sophistication that grants both of them a talent for romantic conflict and conquest.[26] The screwball hero and heroine are both figures adept at the little games and stratagems of the battle of the sexes, and they both take inspiration from past experience in the realm of sexuality.

Unlike the Gothic, where the woman has little sophistication, the screwball heroine is frequently an astute, clever, capable figure of will and self-determination. The screwball heroine is often as strong as – if not stronger than – her male counterpart. More than the Gothic – where the menacing male frequently orchestrates a visual *mise-en-scène* to beguile the helpless heroine – the screwball's realm of manipulation lies in words – in quips, barbs, wisecracks, all of which serve to demonstrate their user's sophisticated savvy, and insofar as the screwball man and woman are both empowered, they equally wield language as an effective weapon in their amorous duel/duet. Indeed, in the screwball, the man is often as disempowered as the woman is in other genres. Screwball heroines are strong-willed, clever figures who frequently push men into a position of emasculinisation or feminisation (see, for instance, Howard Hawks's *Bringing Up Baby* [1938]).

By the end of *Holy Smoke*, much of P. J.'s narrative of control has come undone or been reversed. With the film's constant reversals of power, it is as frequently P. J. who is vulnerable. He has become the swooning figure possessed by romance and is now the one having ecstatic visions (in this case of Ruth as Indian goddess). Most pointedly, if P. J. had early on in the de-programming demarcated himself from Baba as an influence in Ruth's life by noting that, unlike Baba, he doesn't wear a dress, by the end of the film P. J. has undergone a direct feminisation and adopted women's garb (see colour section, between pp.90–1). He has passively allowed Ruth to apply lipstick and rouge to him and put him in a dress, and for a very long (and for some spectators, painful) stretch of the film, he remains in this garb, the romance-struck figure of effusive emotion who cannot live without the other person. Indeed, by the film's end, it might almost seem as if P. J. more appropriately could be awarded the title of 'Gothic heroine': feminised by Ruth, P. J. turns into a veritable lovesick child, awkwardly wandering the desert in his red dress and needing Ruth to come along and save him. He has become a 'damsel-in-distress'. From out of his initial macho position, if P. J. can change, it can only be to go to an opposite extreme: the lovestruck figure of romance.

This is not to say that Ruth fully assumes power in this love duel/duet: *Holy Smoke* is a film of the mutability of power relations, rather than the replacement of one form of power by another. Just as Ruth can immediately recognise P. J.'s cheesy machismo and make emasculating remarks that cut him to the quick, P. J. can see through Ruth's image of self-possession to the insecurities within (he too can stop her cold with a cutting remark). But if Ruth is, as I've already noted, frequently shown to be a figure of immaturity, it is clear too that she possesses an astute quality of perception and expression that gives her power in her interchanges with P. J.

The modesty of *Holy Smoke* has to do then also with a relativising and undercutting of all pretension of character to special strength and status. Ruth and P. J. are ultimately not fairy-tale figures – 'I'm a regular person and you know it,' he tells her – but ordinary people with everyday strengths and weaknesses. (And this is why P. J.'s lovestruck romanticism is ultimately as out-of-place as his cynical machismo; both are too extreme for a modest world where one should calmly go about one's business, including the business of love.) For all its superficial resemblance to a fairy-tale, *Holy Smoke* deflates the tale's otherworldly magic. Significantly, as we've noted, Ruth's infatuation with Baba and his Eastern religion drops away pretty quickly, leaving her with little that she would need to be rescued from (and thereby putting P. J. into a different role than that of the saviour Gothic hero). The house soon becomes less a site of entrapment for Ruth than a space in which she and P. J. both work to break through the other's defences.

But in its last moments, *Holy Smoke* diverges from the ebullient, total optimism of the screwball comedy. In its focus on a man and a woman who are both adept at ploys and the forceful deployment of clever quips, the screwball presents the flowering of romance as a coming together – through reversals of power, but also through compromise – of people of equal nature (even if they had originally seemed at first to be separated by barriers of class, a common theme in the classic screwball) with radiant love emerging out of their ultimate equality. But in updating the screwball comedy to the 1990s, *Holy Smoke* suggests that lovers bring to their rela-

Transit and transport

tionship varying legacies that create differences that can never fully be overcome (for example, Ruth has internalised the lessons of feminism and mocks P. J.'s sexism as something she can never fully accept; likewise, P. J. cannot fully cast off his machismo, and the impossibility of their relationship is signalled when, even though in his red dress, he gives her a sock to the jaw and knocks her out). Both people do learn to evolve but not enough to overcome their differences.

Holy Smoke is in many ways an example of what I termed earlier 'post-national' film-making. For all its resplendent images of the outback (already, however, ones that have a stereotypical status as signs of local colour), the film shows a spatiality in transit, a vulnerable geography of fleeing connection (see colour section, between pp.90–1). This is a film of voyage (to and from India, from and back to the USA), of visceral motion (Ruth driving energetically in her car and exuberantly singing along with a rock song), of a stasis continually interrupted (for all the claustrophobia of the outback house, Ruth and P. J. are constantly being drawn elsewhere, as when the family takes them to a night club). This is film invested in an ever-changing, fleeting world of instability and impossibility of sustained human connection. In such a world, Ruth and P. J. must ultimately go their own ways. Here, again, the film's modesty of ambition becomes part of its subject: there is no transcendental spirit here, no ultimate uplift, and the film can hold out no permanent values (whether of religious devotion or of romantic fulfilment).

Ironically, the film ends with images of Ruth and P. J. having changed for the better, but shows that they have done so not with each other but in new relationships: Ruth has returned to India to help fight poverty there and is with her mother and a new young boyfriend (mentioned almost as an afterthought); P. J. has married his partner Carol (played by 1970s blaxploitation icon Pam Grier) and, like the new sensitive man of the 1990s, is helping to raise their twin babies. Yet Ruth and P. J. admit by letters to each other that they still mean a great deal to each other, and the film ends with a wistfulness at what might have been. In a sense, this is the reverse of the tone of *The Piano*: where the earlier romantic film had ended with an affirmation of the couple interrupted by the reminder of the watery grave that might have been (and that continues to haunt Ada), *Holy Smoke* suggests that it is romance that might have been and that life is to be lived haunted by the regret at what was missed. No doubt there are many reasons why *Holy Smoke* was not a big success – it is too quirky, too inconsistent or undecidable in tone, too modest – but its very structure of an impossible relationship no doubt meant that it could not offer the uplifting affective potential of intense romantic fantasy.

Six
In Progress

In the autumn of 2000, there were official announcements that Campion had begun work on a new film. In the words of an independent film website, 'Miramax and Universal Pictures International announced they will co-finance *In the Cut*, a new thriller starring Nicole Kidman and directed by Jane Campion. Kidman, who is also one of the producers on the project, optioned *In the Cut* from the author Susanna Moore in 1996.'[1]

As this book was going to press, *Variety* for the week 21–27 May 2001 (p. 61), announced that Miramax and Universal had dropped the project and, after going into what the movie business calls 'turnaround', it was picked up by Pathé, the French film company. The article suggests that shooting might start in Autumn 2001 with the film's budget estimated at US$20–30 million.

The novel *In the Cut* is narrated by a female university professor, Frannie, who, when she gets lost in the basement of a bar while looking for the bathroom, witnesses a sex act between a man and a woman. A policeman, Malloy, comes a day later to tell Frannie that the woman was killed later that night, but Frannie notices that the policeman has the same tattoo as the man she saw having sex with the murder victim. While harbouring suspicions about him, Frannie also begins to have strong sexual longings for him, and eventually they begin a sexual relationship. Their sexual encounters are energetic (and described in extremely explicit detail) and frequently have a rough side to them. One review of the novel well captures the dynamics of the relationship:

> Their relationship exists at a strange, unfamiliar emotional register, resembling neither the overluscious passion of the romance novel nor the abject domination/subjugation of porn. Malloy and Frannie exist together like an agreement between thieves, no questions asked and nothing to lose or gain. He is dispassionate, and she refuses to allow him to control the relationship. Yet

> they still seem irrevocably drawn towards one another, she increasingly desperate, he more and more protective. The tone of their interaction is both mistrustful and tender, impersonal and longing, a liaison in which both parties exercise considerable restraint, one out of secrecy, the other out of fear of her lover. Frannie, however, finds her fears and passions grow more and more stronger and uncontrollable, and by the time a second murder occurs, she is overwhelmed by the deeper passions she discovers in herself.[2]

Increasingly, Frannie begins to wonder about all the men in her life and the novel moves toward a frighteningly painful ending in which the killer (who turns out to be Malloy's partner) captures Frannie and begins to torture her to death (an act that bizarrely is described by Frannie herself in first-person narration).

Now, obviously, it is risky to make guesses about future works of a director on the basis of the existing corpus (could anyone have fully imagined *The Piano* from the earlier films?). Interestingly, a review by Peter Rodgers of Moore's novel anticipates Campion's interest in it and suggests a partial affinity of film-maker with this narrative: 'It is as if a Martin Scorsese project starring Joe Mantegna has been given to Jane Campion to interpret, with all the attendant subversions of the genre that might entail.'[3] An article on the new eroticism in films by women directors quotes Campion herself on the project:

> She says the unflinching honest way *In the Cut* deals with female sexuality is what drew her to the Susanna Moore novel. ... What is most disturbing about the book is the suggestion that the woman is seeking her own death. Campion says she will alter the story to remove that suggestion and her movie won't feature real sex, but she speaks admiringly of the novel as 'possibly the most frightening, alarming and erotic piece of literature I've read in a long time. I was actually shocked, frightened by the end of it, really alarmed,' she said in an interview. 'I mean horrified.'[4]

Several aspects of *In the Cut* might be the source of Campion's interest in the project. On the one hand, the novel is quite intensely about the traps that women fall into. Frannie lives in a world of endlessly possible male violence. On the other hand, in a way that has made the novel quite controversial for some feminists, *In the Cut* is also about the ways in which some women may quite deliberately enter into situations fraught with danger. Like Isabel in *The Portrait of a Lady* or Ruth in *Holy Smoke*, Frannie flirts with the very forces that might do her the most harm. There is, as we have seen, a frequent mingling in Campion films of erotic empowerment and willed masochism, that is like Frannie's ease at putting herself in harm's way. As Frannie puts it as she begins a round of rough sex with Malloy (a man she suspects, after all, of being a ruthless killer of women),

> It was as if I had to pretend that I did not know what he was about to do to me. Opening what was closed. Insisting. Fixing me. Unsealing me. At last. I who did not wish to belong to one man. I who did not wish to belong to anyone. I did not want to be fixed, to be pinioned, to be held down. ... I wanted to be fixed, to be pinioned, to be held down.[5]

Clearly, *In the Cut* is no easy and unambiguous work of affirmative, empowering feminism. As such, it reiterates Campion's refusal to produce expected images of women's relation to power. (A revealing anecdote: a professor-friend of mine gave a copy of the book to one of his students who was writing a dissertation, part of which was devoted to Campion. Several days later, she returned it to him with great anger, declaring virulently that it was impossible and even malicious to imagine Jane Campion making a film of such a novel.)

Also controversial for some critics is the novel's representation of race, and, given what we've seen as the debates over the complicated image of racial difference in *The Piano*, it will be interesting to see how a film version might negotiate this fraught area of concern. Frannie is the daughter of a diplomat and spent her childhood in embassies where she was cared for by indigenous women of colour, one of whom is described as an inspiring, virtual mother figure. There is again here the sense of the non-white world as a repository of folk and mythic wisdom for the benefit of whites. Moreover, one of Frannie's students is a young African-American man (whose conversation is rendered frequently in a dialect of 'non-standard' English to signal his difference), and who becomes for her a source both of fear (could he wish her harm?) and of erotic longing: the person of colour becomes, as critics of the novel have suggested, a potential cliché of menace and hyper-sexuality with little agency at the level of communication skills or other 'mainstream' talents. This is not that far from the opening images of *Holy Smoke* in which Ruth, on a crowded bus in India, becomes an image of desire for anonymous men of colour who remain voiceless and inscrutable even as they reach out to the white woman with desire.

It is easy to imagine that, if produced, *In the Cut* will be judged to a large degree in terms of its relation to what people have come to expect from Jane Campion as a director. That is, it may be read either as a film that extends the realm of feminist desire in new directions and opens up bold possibilities for women's self-determination or as one that beneath its chic eroticism replays old stories of female masochism.

Campion's career bears no unity of theme and style but is marked rather by shifts of direction and changes of emphasis. In this respect, this forthcoming project could either affirm existing representations of gender relations in her work or play against them and against viewer expectation.

Conclusion: Rethinking Authorship

The questions raised by Campion's potential projects return us again to the complexity of authorship, and its problematic status as a category for film. Thus, the very project of this book, as all books focused on directors, needs to be reflexive of the category itself – that is, to understand what it can mean to reflect on a career and what the limits of such an approach are to understanding the individual works of a particular director.

How do we draw the boundaries of a career and impute meaning to it?

What, for instance, are we to make of the fact that in 1994, Jane Campion co-wrote a novelisation of *The Piano* with novelist Kate Pullinger? Should this work be treated as an artistic contribution in its own right? Novelisations have long been part of the business of movies, an attempt to extend the appeal of the original work into new markets (as I noted earlier, the screenplay of *The Piano* also appears to have this function insofar as it is not a dry typographical presentation of the script but a sepia-toned romantic object in its own right). There are even recurrent generic features in a novelisation: for instance, there is a close verbal approximation of the film's narrative events, there is frequently an imputation of the emotions the characters would likely be feeling as they lived through these events. Take, for instance, the novel's version of the scene we've analysed of Ada on the cliff looking at her piano:

> [T]he transport party reached a point on the cliff where Ada was afforded a sudden view of the solitary piano against its backdrop of churning sea. She looked down on it, alone in its crate on the wide, comfortless strand, the tide approaching its legs once again. Without her piano she felt very far from home, even farther than she had the night before. She felt voiceless, silenced in a way that had nothing to do with the inability to speak. For several minutes Ada gazed out over the beach, emotions flooding her mind as she struggled to subdue the urge to defy her husband in the first few moments of their marriage. She gripped Flora's hand, anchoring herself to the only thing she had left in the world. She would return, she told herself, she would find a way to retrieve the piano from the beach.[1]

There is little that would not be typical of a novelisation here. But for one detail (in the film, Ada does not grip Flora's hand), the novel finds acceptable verbal approximations of what we see on the screen. And its interpretations of Ada's emotions and thoughts (for example, her resolve to retrieve the piano) – while interpretations certainly – are plausible. All this is in keeping with the established conventions of the novelisation as a genre of writing. We might note that as a verbalisation of narrative actions and allied emotions, the novelisation can render the romantic content of the film's narrative world, but cannot represent the film's visual style. That is, insofar as the romantic style of cinema is rarely linked to a specific character's point of view (as it is, say, when Baines looks through the scrim at the piano in the beams of light) but suffuses the whole film and floats around characters, the novel is of necessity blocked from finding a direct equivalence for the film's romantic visuality. Obviously, for instance, the description of Ada on the cliff cannot describe the out-of-focus look of the background; it cannot mention that the camera's view (but not Ada's) of the piano on the beach is overladen with the diaphanous flutter of her bonnet ribbon. For the novel, the camera – indeed, the cinema overall – cannot be mentioned.

In other words, in its description of scenes and its interpretation of the emotions underlying them, the novelisation of *The Piano* seems a fairly straightforward effort in which there is little attempt to evolve an independent literary style. Its status as an object of authorial criticism – does it deserve a place in the corpus as a creative work? – is ambiguous. (And, we might note, the ambiguity is increased by the novelisation's dual authorship. How was the task of writing divided up? What discussion took place? How were descriptions and interpretations decided upon? Even if, say, Pullinger wrote parts of it alone, would Campion not be considered to have had authorial input insofar as she might have expressed her wishes for how the novel would develop and insofar as Pullinger might in any case have internalised themes and concerns from Campion's film? Where does the influence of an author end? The practical dimensions of authorship are ambiguous and can even go beyond the biological person to others who create in the author's name or tradition.)

But, at other moments, the novelisation of *The Piano* transcends descriptive and interpretative fidelity to what we see on the screen. First of all, we might note that the novelisation frequently interprets emotions and motives in ways that are much more direct and literal than what we see in the film. We might compare the effort here to the film of *The Portrait of a Lady*, which as we've seen is not so much an adaptation as a reworking of James's novel: in particular, the film renders explicit the erotic charge of attraction by emphasising quite palpable, quite tactile acts of kissing. Likewise, *The Piano* novelisation offers up moments of creative rewriting of the film and these frequently involve clarifying explanations of just what the characters are feeling. For example, when Baines brings a piano tuner to his house, we are told that

> George Baines had not traded land and transported the piano to his hut as an object to be merely looked upon in silence; he knew that, with it in tune, Ada McGrath would be unable to resist the instrument. He began to anticipate his next lesson and the opportunity, once again, to be in the presence of Ada McGrath and her uncanny music, which had resonated in his thoughts and dreams since the day at the beach.

Now this is a plausible reading of Baines's feelings at this moment, but it is certainly more interpretively restrictive than what we see on the screen. As I've noted, the film of *The Piano* revels in close-ups of faces – especially of non-speaking faces like Ada's or taciturn ones like Baines's – across which a range of feelings might be intuited. To isolate some emotions or motives out of the panoply of ones possible in the ambiguity of faces is to engage in deliberate resolution of meanings in univocal fashion. The mysteries of the film become the clarity of the novelisation. This, again, raises questions about authorship. What value do we give to Campion's (and Pullinger's) act of reduction? What status do we accord it in explaining the mysteries of the film? (For example, it would be possible to decide that each work has its own independent integrity and that neither has explanatory power over the other.)

The authorial status of the novelisation is further complicated by two other aspects of it that do not follow the film. First, the novel includes a sequence, after Ada's finger has been cut off by Stewart, where Baines has come to say goodbye to his Maori friends (who announce that they are getting ready to fight back with arms against the colonial intruders) and finds that they are in possession of the piano key that Ada had inscribed her love note to Baines upon. Baines takes the key to a nearby school and has the school-children read out the message and then endlessly repeat it to him in what becomes a triumphant celebration of the fact that Ada loves him. This might seem a creative invention for the novel alone, but it is perhaps revealing to note that the screenplay of the film includes the same sequence. In other words, both before *and* after the making of the film itself, Campion seems to have desired this scene; perhaps it was cut from the film for practical reasons (for example, to shorten the film). Just as the explosion of laser disks and videotapes has encouraged an expansive multiplication of newly marketed versions of films through director's cuts, presentations of out-takes and other extensions of the originally released film, so too does Campion's insistence on this sequence, from solely authored screenplay to collaborative novelisation, speak perhaps of an authorial will or desire to imagine another version of the film of *The Piano*. It suggests also that the on-screen film is only one version among several.

Even more ambiguous in its status is the inclusion in the novel of explanations of the primary characters' past, the 'back story'. That is, the novelisation of *The Piano* offers 'flashbacks' in which we learn why Ada fell silent at age six (she was humiliated by her father in front of aunts and had a traumatic reaction); how she got pregnant (her piano teacher slept once with her and then abandoned her); how she was sold to Stewart (in a striking reversal of what we might intuit from the film, we are told that Ada's father sent her to New Zealand to spare her the scandal rather than, as we might expect, to rid himself of a fallen offspring); how Stewart emigrated to New Zealand (too timid in love in Scotland, he decided to remake himself in a new land); how Baines grew up as a whaler and so on. What do we do with these narrative additions? Do we allow them to influence our viewing of the film? Do they become part of its narrative? Do we take pleasure in them for their own sake?[2]

And then if one of the reasons for not looking at *The Piano* novelisation as part of the artistic corpus of the film-maker has to do with the impression that this is not a book of style, not a work that experiments with literary form in a way comparable to Campion's films' play with cinematic style, what do we do with the fact that for *Holy Smoke*, there is also a novelised version, but one that this time does appear to stand as a literary experiment in its own right and makes claims to be read as a worthy part of the corpus (and in fact it was written and published before the making of the film – which could then be seen as its adaptation)?[3] Co-written by Jane Campion with her sister, Anna Campion, who is also a film-maker, the book of *Holy Smoke* is not a standard novelisation (of the sort which sets out to offer a literary record of just what happened in the film and which does not intend to be studied as an artistic object in its own right), but an attempt at a *bona fide* literary work. Indeed, where there is little about the writing of *The Piano* novelisation that would lead one to treat it as a self-sufficient work of literature, the *Holy Smoke* novel was received by some critics as a veritable literary effort and received some journalistic reviews.[4]

Most notable about the novel of *Holy Smoke* is a quite evident play with point of view and with narrational styles: after an epistolary opening in which the Australian therapist contacts P. J. Waters, the exit counsellor, about the young woman Ruth who's joined a cult, the novel bounces back and forth between Ruth's and P. J.'s narration of events and their significance. It might be tempting to add the novelisation of *Holy Smoke* to the Campion corpus as another work to be analysed for theme and style, but, again, questions remain. For example, how do we judge the relative contributions of the two sisters (who, in fact, also collaborated on the screenplay)? How can the director's contributions be disentangled from those of other creative workers? What do we do with the evident fact that this novel was obviously to serve as a production blueprint for the film? Can we say where individual creativity begins or ends? What is an author?[5]

Insofar as such questions suggest instabilities in the notion of authorship, they return us to an understanding of the director's activity as a process of dispersion. Campion's career can seem to centre on *The Piano* as a defining work, but it is also the case that the other works don't condense into mere versions or thematic extensions of that one film. *The Piano* seems to be the extreme incarnation of an emotive and affective cinema of romantic sensibility, and its images of desire, longing and salvation through love came to sum up a particular voice in women's representation. Paradoxically, though, it may be the case that this film is the exception in the director's career even as it comes for many spectators to define it. Both before and after *The Piano*, Campion made painful (if sometimes painfully comic) films about compromise and defeat, films of dashed dreams and desires. Where *The Piano*'s narrative ends with Ada affirming life over death (with, of course, the ambiguity of the final shot back in the grave of the sea which, as we've seen, is taken by some commentators to signal the film's distance from romantic affirmation), other Campion films emphasise the wrong choices, the wrong paths, however unconscious, that characters follow to end up in traps and disillusions. The characters, specifically women, are obsessively blocked by a past in which at some point something went wrong but which is also a source of nostalgia for what could have been (for example, the adult Sweetie stuck on her childhood dreams of stardom) and a source of regret about the compromises that life has entailed. Thus, *Holy Smoke* is, for all its comedy, frequently a sorrowful film: on the one hand, the relationship of Ruth and P. J. resembles more a duel than a love duet (one cannot imagine that these two figures are really destined for each other); on the other hand, this relationship, becomes at the end, an object of wistful nostalgia with the two characters now in relationships that are seen as satisfying but lacking in the love that could have been.

To be sure, *An Angel at My Table*, although a film about a woman frequently entrapped and stifled in her ambitions, is finally an affirmative work, one in which the central character can move into an open future, breaking the blockages that tie her back to the past. Beginning in a very carefully defined milieu, Janet is able to journey beyond the givens of her situation and grow. Towards the film's end, when Janet returns to her family homestead after the death of her father, there is the sense of Janet reconciling with the burden of her past by announcing her difference from it.

But, as I've suggested, Janet's maturation is not presented as specifically organised around the affirmation of romance. To be sure, the adult Janet is able to enter into a relationship (with an American college professor), but this is shown to be an ill-fated affair (one more betrayal of a woman by a man) and eventually becomes no more than an interlude with little impact on the real core of Janet's growth: her recognition that she best establishes herself, her being, by the act of writing. At the end of the film, Janet dances alone in the night and then goes into her trailer to sit at her typewriter. Solitude has now become the site of her self-affirmation. Aesthetic creation has become her life.

In contrast, *The Piano*'s narrative implies that a fixation on one's art can impede growth. Ada has to learn to transfer her affections from her piano to a man. One's being finds fulfilment in a fundamental act of sociality, of linking one's destiny to another. This is quite different from the isolation or the relationships, compromised at best, that characters live through in the other films: the distance in the relationship between Kay and Louis in *Sweetie*, the family atomised in *Peel*, the people caught up in their own individualised foibles in the aptly named *Passionless Moments*, Janet in her solitude (no matter how uplifting), Isabel in her traps and frozen at the film's end, P. J. and Ruth living the compromises of new relationships tinged with nostalgia and regret.

It may be then that it is precisely the complication of Jane Campion's career in relation to notions of auteurism that makes her work most interesting. With one film that has attained canonical status and a range of earlier works that received esteem in art-film venues, she is one of very few women directors who could be considered within the framework of auteurism. Yet it is the disturbances in her work – the divergences; the dispersions; the tensions, for instance, between quirky humour, a making strange of the familiar, and an interest in the ambiguous, even that which is uncomfortable and which makes the viewer uncomfortable – that means that to study her is to study the cinema differently, to rethink the very terms of analysis of the film director. There is in her films a combination of attraction and of deliberate discomfort. As can be seen in the divergent responses to *The Piano*, Campion's films have the capacity to seduce viewers, yet also to disrupt that seduction by refusing to present unambiguously positive representations of human relations, in particular those of women to the social world around them.

NOTES

1 – Resonant Melodies

1. 'Interview with Gerard Lee and John Maynard', *Cinema Papers*, no. 106, October 1995, p. 6.
2. In her short book on Jane Campion, Ellen Cheshire offers additional examples of the resonance of *The Piano* in popular culture:

   > The film has taken on a life beyond its original intention, it has entered into the mass media and has been quoted and referenced usually humorously in TV and films as diverse as French and Saunders' lampooning of the film in their BBC Television series and in the US TV series *Friends*. Joey tries to chat up a young lady ... in a video shop by claiming he is about to rent *The Piano*. However, she is not impressed as she's renting an action flick. In Tom DiCillo's 1997 film *The Real Blonde*, one of the film's few memorable scenes sees an entire restaurant debating the merits or otherwise of *The Piano*. Opinions in the restaurant scene include: 'great great movie', 'piece of shit', 'courage, freedom, unrestricted and unconditional primal love', 'what the hell was that movie about?', 'I liked Harvey Keitel's ass', 'great photography', and 'that little girl bugged me, if I had a daughter like that I'd kick her butt.'

   See Ellen Cheshire, *The Pocket Essential Jane Campion* (Harpenden: Pocket Essentials, 2000), p. 54.
3. US and UK figures come from the Internet Movie Database (www.imdb.com), www.worldwideboxoffice.com, and box-office data services such as Paul Kagan Associates, Inc. and Hollywood Pro, and may not be official or fully accurate (indeed, there are slight discrepancies from accounting company to company). But I do think they are indicative of overall trends in the returns to the various works. Australian figures come from the Australian Film Commission, and I thank the Commission's Research Manager, Rosemary Curtis, for providing me with this information. Theo van Leeuwen notes also that the compact disc of the film's score was likewise a phenomenal success:

   > This is music to express the inexpressible, the damned-up emotions that have no outlet, and it has pulled the heartstrings of viewers the world over, as evidenced by the phenomenal success of the soundrack CD: the recording was number one in the classical and 'crossover' charts in the USA and number 519 in the pop charts, and sold 700,000 copies worldwide.

   See Theo van Leeuwen, 'Emotional Times: The Music of *The Piano*', in Rebecca Coyle (ed.), *Screen Scores: Studies in Contemporary Australian Screen Music* (New South Wales: Australian Film, Television and Radio School, 1998), p. 41.

2 – Desiring the Director

1. Toby Miller and Noel King, 'Auteurism in the 1990s', in Pam Cook and Mieke Bernink (eds), *The Cinema Book* (London: BFI, 1999), p. 315.

2. Judith Mayne, *Directed by Dorothy Arzner* (Bloomington, IN: Indiana University Press, 1994).
3. Michel Foucault, 'What is an Author?', in Donald F. Bouchard (ed.), *Language, Counter-Memory, Practice* (Ithaca, NY: Cornell University Press, 1977), pp. 113–38.
4. Thomas Elsaesser, 'The Road to Morocco: Bergman, Art Cinema, and Beyond', *Aura*, vol. 6, no. 3, 2000, p. 10.
5. See, for instance, David Bordwell, *On the History of Film Style* (Cambridge, MA: Harvard University Press, 1998).
6. Roland Barthes, *Mythologies*, trans. Annette Lavers (New York: Hill and Wang, 1972), p. 112.
7. Foucault, 'What is an Author?', p. 123.
8. Carol Clover, 'Ecstatic Mutilation', *The Threepenny Review*, no. 57, 1994, p. 20.
9. Tino Balio, 'The Art Film Market in the New Hollywood', in Geoffrey Nowell-Smith and Steven Ricci (eds), *Hollywood and Europe: Economics, Culture, National Identity* (London: BFI, 1998), p. 66.
10. Elsaesser, 'The Road to Morocco', p. 10.
11. Peter Calder, 'Would-Be Warriors: New Zealand Film since *The Piano*', in Jonathan Dennis and Jan Bieringa (eds), *Film in Aotearoa, New Zealand* (Wellington, NZ: Victoria University Press, 1996), 2nd edn, p. 184.
12. Tom O'Regan, *Australian National Cinema* (London and New York: Routledge, 1996), p. 72.
13. Steven Neale, 'Art Cinema as Institution', *Screen*, vol.22, no. 1, Spring 1981, pp. 11–39.

3 – Dividing Lines

1. See www.fys.uio.no/magnushj/Piano/opinion.html
2. Vivian Sobchack, 'What My Fingers Knew: The Cinesthetic Subject, or Vision in the Flesh', in *Carnal Thoughts: Bodies, Texts, Scenes and Screens* (Berkeley: Univ. of California Press, forthcoming).
3. Freda Freiberg, 'The Bizarre in the Banal: Notes on the Films of Jane Campion', in Annette Blonski, Barbara Creed and Freda Freiberg (eds), *Don't Shoot Darling! Women's Independent Film-Making in Australia* (Richmond, Australia: Greenhouse, 1987), pp. 328–33.
4. Rick Altman, *Film/Genre* (London: BFI, 1999).
5. Laleen Jayamanne, 'Post-Colonial Gothic: The Narcissistic Wound of Jane Campion's *The Piano*', *Towards Cinema and its Double: Cross-Cultural Readings, 1981–1999* (Bloomington, IN: Indiana University Press, forthcoming).
6. Dryburgh, quoted in Jane Campion, *The Piano* (London: Bloomsbury, 1993; New York: Hyperion/Miramax Books, 1993), p. 141.
7. Henry James, *The Portrait of a Lady* (London and New York: Penguin Classics, 1986 [1881]), p. 403.
8. See Donald Williams, '*The Piano*: The Isolated, Constricted Self', *The C. G. Jung Page*, www.cgjung.com/films/pianox.html/; and John Izod, '*The Piano*, the Animus, and Colonial Experience', in Harriet Margolis (ed.), *Jane Campion's The Piano* (Cambridge and New York: Cambridge University Press, 2000), pp. 86–113.

9. Cynthia Kaufman, 'Colonialism, Purity, and Resistance in *The Piano*', *Socialist Review*, vol. 24, nos. 1–2, 1995, pp. 252–3. For other applications of Kristeva to *The Piano*, see Chella Courington, 'Woolf through the Lens of Campion: *The Piano* and *The Voyage Out*', in Deborah Cartmell, I. Q. Hunter, Heidi Kaye and Imelda Whelehan (eds), *Sisterhoods: Across the Literature/Media Divide* (London and Virginia: Pluto Press, 1998), pp. 136–48; and Richard Allen, 'Female Sexuality, Creativity, and Desire in *The Piano*', in Felicity Coombs and Suzanne Gemmell (eds), *Piano Lessons: Approaches to the Piano* (Sydney: John Libbey & Co., 1999), pp. 44–63. (This essay was originally published in *Psychoanalytic Psychology*, 17, no. 2, 1995, pp. 185–201.)
10. The cyclicity of the woman's film is discussed by feminist film theorist Tania Modleski in a classic essay, 'Time and Desire in the Woman's Film', *Cinema Journal*, vol. 23, no. 3, Spring 1984, pp. 19–30.
11. For a direct comparison of *The Piano* to *Letter from an Unknown Woman*, see Neil Robinson, 'With Choices Like These, Who Needs Enemies?: *The Piano*, Women's Articulations, Melodrama, and the Woman's Film', in Coombs and Gemmell (eds), *Piano Lessons*, pp. 19–43.
12. Jocelyn Robson and Beverly Zalcock, *Girl's Own Stories: Australian and New Zealand Women's Films* (London: Scarlet Press, 1997), pp. 11–12. Another study of Australian cinema as an indigenisation of British and classic Hollywood forms is Brian McFarlane and Geoff Mayer, *New Australian Cinema: Sources and Parallels in American and British Film* (Cambridge: Cambridge University Press, 1992).
13. For background, see my *Power and Paranoia: History, Narrative, and the American Cinema, 1940–1950* (New York: Columbia University Press, 1986), pp. 277–89.
14. Claire Corbett, 'Cutting It Fine: Notes on *The Piano* in the Editing Room', in Coombs and Gemmell (eds), *Piano Lessons*, p. 165.
15. Susan Faludi, *Stiffed: The Betrayal of the American Man* (New York: William Morrow and Co., 1999).
16. Tania Modleski, 'Axe the Piano Player', in *Old Wives Tales and Other Women's Stories* (New York and London: New York University Press, 1999), pp. 37–8.
17. Naomi Segal, 'The Fatal Attraction of *The Piano*', in Nicholas White and Naomi Segal (eds), *Scarlet Letters: Fictions of Adultery from Antiquity to the 1990s* (London: Macmillan, 1997), p. 208.
18. Carol Jacobs, 'Playing Jane Campion's *Piano*: Politically', *MLN*, no. 109, 1994, p. 760.
19. Laura Mulvey, 'Visual Pleasure and Narrative Cinema' (1975), reprinted in Mulvey, *Visual and Other Pleasures* (London: BFI, 1989), p. 26.
20. Stella Bruzzi, 'Tempestuous Petticoats: Costume and Desire in *The Piano*', *Screen*, vol. 36, no. 3, Autumn 1995, p. 257.
21. Ibid., p. 261.
22. Leonie Pihama, 'Are Films Dangerous? A Maori Woman's Perspective on *The Piano*', *Hecate*, vol. 20, no. 2, October 1994, pp. 239–42.

23. Anna Neill, 'A Land without a Past: Dreamtime and Nation in *The Piano*', in Coombs and Gemmell (eds), *Piano Lessons*, p. 138.
24. Kaufman, 'Colonialism, Purity, and Resistance in *The Piano*', pp. 253–4.
25. Ibid., p. 254.
26. Ibid.
27. Sue Gillett, 'Lips and Fingers: Jane Campion's *The Piano*', *Screen*, vol. 36, no. 3, Summer 1995, p. 281.
28. Kerryn Goldsworthy, 'What Music Is', *Arena Magazine*, no. 7, October–November 1993, pp. 46–8; and Lisa Sarmas, 'What Rape Is', *Arena Magazine*, no. 8, December 1993–January 1994, p. 14. Further references to Goldsworthy are provided in the text.

4 – Beginnings: Intention and Method

1. 'Fresh Air Interview with Terry Gross', National Public Radio, 11 April 2000; www.npr.org
2. I piece together the key points in Campion's early biography from articles, websites and above all the collection of Campion interviews edited by Virginia Wright Wexman (see Select Bibliography).
3. Mark Stiles, 'Jane Campion', in Virginia Wright Wexman (ed.), *Jane Campion: Interviews* (Jackson: University Press of Mississippi, 1999), pp. 4–5.
4. Thomas Bourguinon and Michel Ciment, 'Interview with Jane Campion: More Barbarian than Aesthete', in Wright Wexman (ed.), *Jane Campion: Interviews*, p. 102.
5. Campion recounts some of her Cannes experience in 'Notes from a Broad', *Xpress* (Australia), no. 5, August–October 1986, pp. 10–11. Rissient discusses his scouting efforts on behalf of Australian film in an interview with the Australian journal, *Cinema Papers*, no. 79, May 1990, pp. 48–53. Significantly, Rissient argues that there has been a worldwide decline in the quality of works from national cinemas, but singles out Campion for 'idiosyncratic' qualities that for him separate her off from the general tendencies of Australian film.
6. Roger Ebert, Review of *Sweetie*, *Chicago Sun Times*, 23 March 1990; www.suntimes.com/ebert/ebert_reviews/1990/03/537986.html
7. Mary Colbert, 'Sally Bongers: cinematographer particulaire', *Cinema Papers*, no. 75, September 1989, p. 5.
8. Ibid., pp. 5–6.
9. Ibid., p. 7.
10. Clover, 'Ecstatic Mutilation', pp. 20–2
11. Pam Cook, '*Passionless Moments*', *Monthly Film Bulletin*, vol. 57, no. 678, July 1990, p. 210.
12. 'Different Complexions: an Interview with Miro Bilbrough', in Dennis and Bieringa (eds), *Film in Aotearoa, New Zealand*, p. 101.
13. See Gina Hausknecht, 'Self-Possession, Dolls, Beatlemania, Loss: Telling the Girl's Own Story', in Ruth O. Saxton (ed.), *The Girl: Constructions of the Girl in Contemporary Fiction by Women* (New York: St Martin's Press, 1998), pp. 21–42.
14. Freiberg, 'The Bizarre in the Banal: Notes on the Films of Jane Campion', pp. 330–1.

15. Ibid.
16. Helen Garner, *The Last Days of Chez Nous & Two Friends* (Victoria: Penguin Books Australia, 1992).
17. Michel Ciment, 'Two Interviews with Jane Campion', in Wright Wexman (ed.), *Jane Campion: Interviews*, p. 35.
18. Ibid., p. 36.
19. Anneke Smelik, 'The Gothic Image', *And the Mirror Cracked: Feminist Cinema and Film Theory* (New York: St Martin's Press, 1998), p. 139.
20. David Stratton, 'An Interview with Jane Campion', in Gerard Lee and Jane Campion, *Sweetie: The Screenplay* (Saint Lucia: University of Queensland Press, 1991), p. xi.
21. Smelik, 'The Gothic Image', pp. 142–3.
22. Ibid., p. 150.
23. See Helen Martin and Sam Edwards, *New Zealand Film, 1912–1996* (London and New York: Oxford University Press, 1997), p. 148.
24. Sue Gillett, 'Angel from the Mirror City: Jane Campion's Janet Frame', *Senses of Cinema*, no. 10, November 2000; www.sensesofcinema.com/contents/00/10/angel.html

5 – After-Shocks

1. Vicky Roach, 'Campion Takes on Spielberg at His Game', in Wright Wexman (ed.), *Jane Campion: Interviews*, p. 173.
2. Vincent Ostria and Thierry Jousse, '*The Piano*: Interview with Jane Campion', in ibid., p. 132.
3. Michel Ciment, 'A Voyage to Discover Herself', in ibid., p. 181.
4. Laura Jones, *The Portrait of a Lady: Screenplay* (London and New York: Penguin Books, 1996), p. vi.
5. 'Nervous in Venice', *Daily Telegraph* (Australia), 7 September 1996, p. 25.
6. Jones, *The Portrait of a Lady: Screenplay*, p. 1.
7. William E. Shriver, review of *The Portrait of a Lady*, *Movie Hotline*; www.amesev.net/movies/reviews/portrait.html
8. Linda DeLiberio, 'Girlie Shows', *In the Arts*, vol. 21, no. 7, 17 February 1997, p. 30.
9. Brian McFarlane, '*The Portrait of a Lady*', *Cinema Papers*, no. 115, April 1998,p. 37.
10. Quoted in Ric Gentry, 'Painterly Touches' (interview with Stuart Dryburgh), *American Cinematographer*, vol. 78, no. 1, January 1997, p. 55.
11. Ibid., pp. 55–6.
12. Ibid., p. 52.
13. Ibid.
14. Ibid.
15. James, *The Portrait of a Lady*, pp. 120–1.
16. Jones, *The Portrait of a Lady: Screenplay*, p. 8.
17. Kathleen Murphy, 'Jane Campion's Passage to India' (essay with interpolated comments by Jane Campion), *Film Comment*, vol. 36, no. 1, January–February 2000, p. 30.
18. See, for instance, Adrian Martin, 'Losing the Way: The Decline of Jane Campion', *Landfall* (NZ), no. 200, November 2000, pp. 89–102 which very explicitly argues a major decline in Campion's work.
19. Bernard Weinraub, 'At the Movies', *New York Times*, 3 December 1999, p. E22.
20. Maxine McKew, 'Jane Campion and *Holy Smoke*' (interview), *ABC 7:30 Report* (Australia), 13 December 1999, www.abc.net.au/7.30/stories/s73088.htm

21. Anna Campion, 'Scenes from a Dreamtime Odyssey', *Sunday Herald-Sun*, 1st edn, 30 January 2000, p. Z16.
22. Sean Axmaker, '*Holy Smoke*', *Nitrate Online Review*, 20 October 2000; www.nitrateonline.com/1999/rholysmoke.html
23. Gary Mairs, '*Holy Smoke*', Culturevulture.net; culturevulture.net/Movies/ HolySmoke.html.
24. See Andrew L. Urban, 'Hallucination F/X' (interview with *Holy Smoke*'s digital effects supervisor), *Urban Cinefile*; www.urbancinefile.com.au/home/article_view.asp?Article_ID=2836
25. I advance this argument in depth in *In a Lonely Place* (London: BFI, 1993).
26. See Stanley Cavell, *Pursuits of Happiness: The Hollywood Comedy of Remarriage* (Cambridge, MA: Harvard University Press, 1981).

6 – In Progress

1. See www.indiewire.com/film/biz/biz_991110_briefs.html
2. See 'Beyond *Basic Instinct*'; www.chronicle.duke.edu/story.php?article_id=5038
3. Peter Rodgers, review of *In the Cut*; www.richmondreview.co.uk/books/inthecut.html
4. Eric Harrison, 'Women Film-Makers Put the X in Sex', *Houston Chronicle* (2000), www.chron.com.
5. Susanna Moore, *In the Cut* (New York: Alfred A. Knopf, 1995), p. 118.

Conclusion: Rethinking Authorship

1. Jane Campion and Kate Pullinger, *The Piano* (New York: Hyperion/Miramax Books, 1994), pp. 31–2.
2. Ken Gelder analyses the novelisation in 'Jane Campion and the Limits of Literary Cinema', in Deborah Cartmell and Imelda Whelehan (eds), *Adaptations: From Text to Screen, Screen to Text* (London and New York: Routledge, 1999), pp. 164–8. As Gelder puts it, the novel is 'in a secondary, slighter role as something less than the film. The novel's project is first and foremost to explain rather than to allow the imagination a free, "unfettered" rein, not "Show, don't tell!" but "Tell, don't show!" It thus completes a film which had valorised incompleteness, and in so doing it runs the risk of saying too much' (pp. 164–5). Gelder quotes from an interview with the novel's co-writer, Kate Pullinger, in which she indicates her own dissatisfaction at the assignment: '[Pullinger] was ... restrained by Campion's first chapters, which covered Ada's motherlessness, her father's decaying estate, her life until the age of sixteen, and her music teacher – and restrained again by her willingness to fax pages to Campion for amending, then picking up with the details as Campion saw them' (p. 164).
3. Anna and Jane Campion, *Holy Smoke* (New York: Hyperion, 1999).
4. See, for instance, the review by G. Turner in the Books section of the *Sunday Mail* (Queensland), 2nd edn, 27 June 1999.
5. Along with these theoretical issues about what influence and contribution are in the production of a film, it is necessary to note that there have also been some very direct and practical questions raised

about the originality of *The Piano* as an authored work. Towards the end of the 1990s, controversy arose about the originality of the narrative premise and unfolding of *The Piano*. In the 1920s, there had been a novel by Jane Mander, *The Story of a New Zealand River*, that also dealt with a European woman who comes to New Zealand with her piano and her daughter and begins an affair with another man than her husband some critics came close to accusing Campion of taking many ideas from this story. Campion had in the past admitted knowledge of the novel – and even at times some inspiration from it – but at least one scholar, Diane Hoeveler writing in *Literature/Film Quarterly*, argued that the similarities between the two works seemed more than accidental. See Diane L. Hoeveler, 'Silence, Sex, and Feminism: An Examination of *The Piano*'s Unacknowledged Sources', *Literature/Film Quarterly*, vol. 26, no. 2, 1998, pp. 109–16. *The Oxford Companion to Australian Film* went so far as to claim that the film was directly based on Mander's novel although the film did not credit this source. Later, in response to protests from Campion and her agent, the editors at Oxford removed the claim from the volume. Meanwhile, a journalist found a letter from Campion in 1985 that appeared to indicate that in response to an offer to adapt the novel to the screen, Campion had directly stated that Mander's novel was the inspiration for her own script-in-progress, *The Piano Lesson*. For some, this seemed to confirm that Campion's knowledge of the Mander book was more than casual. There were also charges that Campion had paid money to the Jane Mander estate to compensate for her film having made a direct adaptation of Mander's novel a less viable project. Some critics of Campion even demanded that she be forced to give back her Best Original Screenplay Oscar, but the controversy finally seemed to die down without full resolution. For a summary, see Hillary Frey, 'Purloined Piano?', *Lingua Franca*, vol. 10, no. 6, September 2000, pp. 8–10.

SELECT BIBLIOGRAPHY

General Works on Jane Campion

Bloustein, Geraldine. 'Jane Campion: Memory, Motif and Music', *Continuum*, vol. 5, no. 2, 1992, pp. 29–39.

Campion, Jane. 'Big Shell' (short story), *Rolling Stone Yearbook 1988* (Australian edn), pp. 72–4.

Campion, Jane. 'Different Complexions: an Interview with Miro Bilbrough', in Jonathan Dennis and Jan Bieringa (eds), *Film in Aotearoa, New Zealand* (Wellington, NZ: Victoria University Press, 1992; 1996), pp. 93–104.

Campion, Jane. 'Le Pli' (short story, trans. Pierre Berthomieu), *Positif*, no. 444, February 1998, pp.79–84.

Cheshire, Ellen. *The Pocket Essential Jane Campion* (Harpenden: Pocket Essentials, 2000).

Freiberg, Freda. 'The Bizarre in the Banal: Notes on the Films of Jane Campion', in Annette Blonski, Barbara Creed and Freda Freiberg (eds), *Don't Shoot Darling! Women's Independent Film-Making in Australia* (Richmond, Australia: Greenhouse, 1987), pp. 328–33.

Gelder, Ken. 'Jane Campion and the Limits of Literary Cinema', in Deborah Cartmell and Imelda Whelehan (eds), *Adaptations: From Text to Screen, Screen to Text* (London and New York: Routledge, 1999), pp. 157–71.

Gillett, Sue. 'A Pleasure to Watch: Jane Campion's Narrative Cinema', *Screening the Past*, March 2001; www.latrobe.edu.au/www/screeningthepast/firstrelease/fr0301/sgfr12a.htm

Martin, Adrian. 'Losing the Way: The Decline of Jane Campion', *Landfall* (NZ), no. 200, November 2000, pp. 89–102.

McHugh, Kathleen. 'Sounds that Creep Inside You: Female Narration and Voiceover in the Films of Jane Campion', forthcoming, *Style*, Summer 2001.

Mellencamp, Pat. 'Jane Campion', *A Fine Romance: Five Ages of Film Feminism* (Philadelphia: Temple University Press, 1995), pp. 173–83.

Redding, Judith M. and Victoria A. Brownsworth. 'Jane Campion: A Girl's Own Story', *Films Fatales: Independent Women Directors* (Seattle, WA: Seal Press, 1997), pp. 179–84.

Robson, Jocelyn and Beverly Zalcock. *Girl's Own Stories: Australian and New Zealand Women's Films* (London: Scarlet Press, 1997).

Slavin, John. 'The Films of Jane Campion', *Metro*, 95, 1993, pp. 28–30.

Taylor, Ella. 'Jane Campion', *LA Weekly*, 14–20 June 2000, pp. 20–5.

Wright Wexman, Virginia (ed.). *Jane Campion: Interviews* (Jackson: University Press of Mississippi, 1999).

Peel

Paskin, Sylvia. '*Peel*', *Monthly Film Bulletin*, vol. 57, no. 678, July 1990, pp. 210–11.

Passionless Moments

Cook, Pam. '*Passionless Moments*', *Monthly Film Bulletin*, vol. 57, no. 678, July 1990, p. 210.

A Girl's Own Story

Glaessner, Verina. '*A Girl's Own Story*', *Monthly Film Bulletin*, vol. 57, no. 678, July 1990, p. 209.

Hausknecht, Gina. 'Self-Possession, Dolls, Beatlemania, Loss: Telling the Girl's Own Story', in Ruth O. Saxton (ed.), *The Girl: Constructions of the Girl in Contemporary Fiction by Women* (New York: St Martin's Press, 1998), pp. 21–42.

Two Friends

Garner, Helen. *The Last Days of Chez Nous & Two Friends* (Victoria: Penguin Books Australia, 1992).

Hawker, Philippa. 'A Tale of Friendships and … a Few Little Surprises' (interview with Helen Garner), *The Age*, 24 April 1986.

Sweetie

Gillett, Sue. 'More Than Meets the Eye: The Mediation of Affects in Jane Campion's *Sweetie*', *Senses of Cinema*, no. 1, December 1999; www.sensesofcinema.com/contents/00/1/sweetie.html

Lee, Gerard and Jane Campion. *Sweetie: The Screenplay* (Saint Lucia: University of Queensland Press, 1991).

Smelik, Anneke. 'The Gothic Image', *And the Mirror Cracked: Feminist Cinema and Film Theory* (New York: St Martin's Press, 1998), pp. 139–51.

Strain, Ellen. 'Reinstating the Cultural Framework: Kay Shaffer's *Women and the Bush* and Jane Campion's *Sweetie*', *Spectator*, vol. 11, no. 2, 1991, pp. 32–43.

An Angel at My Table

Frame, Janet. *An Autobiography* (New York: George Braziller, Inc., 1991).

Gillett, Sue. 'Angel from the Mirror City: Jane Campion's Janet Frame', *Senses of Cinema*, no. 10, November 2000; www.sensesofcinema.com/contents/00/10/angel.html.

Henke, Suzette A. 'Jane Campion Frames Janet Frame: A Portrait of the Artist as a Young New Zealand Poet', *Biography*, vol. 23, no. 4, 2000, pp. 651–69.

The Piano

Althofer, Beth. '*The Piano*, or *Wuthering Heights* Revisited, or Separation and Civilization through the Eyes of the (Girl) Child', *Psychoanalytic Review*, vol. 8, no. 2, Summer 1994, pp. 339–42.

Attwood, Feona. 'Weird Lullaby: Jane Campion's *The Piano*', *Feminist Review*, no. 58, Spring 1998, pp. 85–101.

Baker, David. 'Mud-Wrestling with the Angels: *The Piano* as Literature', *Southern Review* (Australia), vol. 30, no. 2, 1997, pp. 180–201.

Bell, Philip. 'All that Patriarchy Allows: The Melodrama of *The Piano*', *Metro* (Australia), no. 102, May 1995, pp. 57–60.

Bird, Carmel. 'Freedom of Speech', in Cassandrus Pybus (ed.), *Columbus's Blindness and Other Essays* (Saint Lucia: University of Queensland Press, 1994), pp. 190–8.

Bruzzi, Stella. 'Bodyscape' (with inserts of comments from *The Piano*'s crew), *Sight and Sound*, vol. 3, no. 10, October 1993, pp. 6–10.

Bruzzi, Stella. 'Tempestuous Petticoats: Costume and Desire in *The Piano*', *Screen*, vol. 36, no. 3, Autumn 1995, pp. 257–66.

Bruzzi, Stella. *Undressing Cinema: Clothing and Identity in the Movies* (London and New York: Routledge, 1997), pp. 57–63.

Campion, Jane. *The Piano* (screenplay) (London: Bloomsbury , 1993; New York: Hyperion/Miramax Books, 1993).

Campion, Jane and Kate Pullinger. *The Piano* (novelisation) (New York: Hyperion/Miramax Books, 1994).

Chomo II, Peter. 'Keys to the Imagination: Jane Campion's *The Piano*', *Literature/Film Quarterly*, vol. 25, no. 3, 1997, pp. 173–6.

Clover, Carol. 'Ecstatic Mutilation', *The Threepenny Review*, no. 57, 1994, pp. 20–2.

Coombs, Felicity and Suzanne Gemmell (eds). *Piano Lessons: Approaches to The Piano* (Sydney: John Libbey & Co., 1999).

Courington, Chella. 'Woolf through the Lens of Campion: *The Piano* and *The Voyage Out*', in Deborah Cartmell, I. Q. Hunter, Heidi Kaye and Imelda Whelehan (eds), *Sisterhoods: Across the Literature/Media Divide* (London and Virginia: Pluto Press, 1998), pp. 136–48.

Dapkus, Jeanne R. 'Sloughing Off the Burdens: Parallel/Antithetical Quests for Self-Actualisation', *Literature/Film Quarterly*, vol. 25, no. 3, 1997, pp. 177–87.

Depardieu, Alain. 'Les Notes de *La Leçon de Piano*' (production diary), *Studio Magazine*, December 1993, pp. 105–7.

Dyson, Linda. 'The Return of the Repressed: Whiteness, Femininity and Colonialism in *The Piano*', *Screen*, vol. 36, no. 3, Summer 1995, pp. 267–76.

Eckman-Jadow, Judith. '*The Piano*, A Re-Visit to the "Dark Continent"', *Issues in Psychoanalytic Psychology*, vol. 17, no. 2, 1995, pp. 202–16.

Gillett, Sue. 'Lips and Fingers: Jane Campion's *The Piano*', *Screen*, vol. 36, no. 3, Summer 1995, pp. 277–87.

Goldson, Annie. 'Piano Lessons', in Jonathan Dennis and Jan Bieringa (eds), *Film in Aotearoa, New Zealand* (Wellington, NZ: Victoria University Press, 1992; 1996), pp. 195–8.

Goldson, Annie. '*Piano* Recital', *Screen*, vol. 38, no. 3, Autumn 1997, pp. 275–81.

Goldsworthy, Kerryn. 'What Music Is', *Arena Magazine*, no. 7, October–November 1993, pp. 46–8.

Gordon, Suzy. 'I Clipped Your Wing, That's All': Auto-eroticism and the Female Spectator in *The Piano*', *Screen*, vol. 37, no. 2, Summer 1996, pp. 193–205.

Greenberg, Harvey. '*The Piano*', *Film Quarterly*, vol. 47, no. 3, Spring 1994, pp. 46–50.

Hazel, Valerie. 'Disjointed Articulations: The Politics of Vision and Jane Campion's *The Piano*', *Women's Studies Journal*, vol. 10, no. 2, September 1994, pp. 27–40.

Hendershot, Cyndy. '(Re)Visioning the Gothic: Jane Campion's *The Piano*', *Literature/Film Quarterly*, vol. 26, no. 2, 1998, pp. 97–108.

Hoeveler, Diane L. 'Silence, Sex, and Feminism: An Examination of *The Piano*'s Unacknowledged Sources', *Literature/Film Quarterly*, vol. 26, no. 2, 1998, pp. 109–16.

Jayamanne, Laleen. 'Post-Colonial Gothic: The Narcissistic Wound of Jane Campion's *The Piano*', *Towards Cinema and its Double: Cross-Cultural Readings, 1981–1999* (Bloomington, IN: Indiana University Press, forthcoming).

Jones, Stan. 'Ecstasies in the Mossy Land: New Zealand Film in Germany', in Deb Verhoeven (ed.), *Twin Peeks: Australian & New Zealand Film* (Victoria: Australia Catalogue Company Ltd, 1999), pp. 151–70.

Kaufman, Cynthia. 'Colonialism, Purity, and Resistance in *The Piano*', *Socialist Review*, vol. 24, nos. 1–2, 1995, pp. 251–5.

Margolis, Harriet (ed.). *Jane Campion's The Piano* (Cambridge and New York: Cambridge University Press, 2000).

Modleski, Tania. 'Axe the Piano Player', in *Old Wives Tales and Other Women's Stories* (New York and London: New York University Press, 1999), pp. 31–46.

Molina, Caroline. 'Muteness and Mutilation: The Aesthetics of Disability in Jane Campion's *The Piano*', in David T. Mitchell and Sharon L. Snyder (eds), *The Body and Physical Difference: Discourses of Disability* (Ann Arbor, MI: University of Michigan Press, 1997), pp. 267–82.

Perkins, Reid. 'Imag(in)ing Our Colonial Past: Colonial New Zealand on Film from *The Birth of New Zealand* to *The Piano* (part II), *Illusions*, no.26, Winter 1997, pp. 17–21.

Pihama, Leonie. 'Are Films Dangerous? A Maori Woman's Perspective on *The Piano*', *Hecate*, vol. 20, no. 2, October 1994, pp. 239–42.

Reid, Mark A. 'A Few Black Keys and Maori Tattoos: Re-Reading Jane Campion's *The Piano* in PostNegritude Time', *Quarterly Review of Film and Video*, vol. 17, no. 2, June 2000, pp. 107–16.

Riley, Vikki. 'Ancestor Worship: The Earthly Paradise of Jane Campion's Universe', *Metro* (Australia), no. 102, May 1995, pp. 61–3.

Roth, Bennett E. '*The Piano*: A Modern Film Melodrama About Crime and Punishment', *Psychoanalytic Psychology*, vol. 17, no. 2, 2000, pp. 405–13.

Sarmas, Lisa. 'What Rape Is', *Arena Magazine*, no. 8, December 1993–January 1994, p. 14.

Segal, Naomi. 'The Fatal Attraction of *The Piano*', in Nicholas White and Naomi Segal (eds), *Scarlet Letters: Fictions of Adultery from Antiquity to the 1990s* (London: Macmillan, 1997), pp. 199–211.

Thornley, Davinia. 'Duel or Duet?: Gendered Nationalism in *The Piano*', *Film Criticism*, vol. 24, no. 3, Spring 2000, pp. 61–76.

Urban, Andrew L. 'Making of: *The Piano*' (includes interview with Jane Campion), *Urban Cinefile*; www.urbancinefile.com.au/home/article_view.asp?Article_ID=1512

Van Buren, Jane. 'Silences from the Deep: Mapping Being and Nonbeing in *The Piano* and in a Schizoid Young Woman', *The American Journal of Psychoanalysis*, vol. 60, no. 2, June 2000, pp. 139–61.

Van Leeuwen, Theo. 'Emotional Times: The Music of *The Piano*', in Rebecca Coyle (ed.), *Screen Scores: Studies in Contemporary Australian Screen Music* (New South Wales: Australian Film, Television and Radio School, 1998), pp. 39–48.

Williams, Donald. '*The Piano*: The Isolated, Constricted Self', *The C. G. Jung Page*; www.cgjungpage.org

The Portrait of a Lady

Andrew, Geoff. '*Portrait of a Lady*', *Time Out* (January 1996); available at www.nicolekidman.org/articles/9601-timeout.asp

Axelrad, Catherine.'Portrait de femme: La femme peintre et son modèle', *Positif*, no. 430, December 1996, pp. 9–10.

Bauer, Dale M. 'Jane Campion's Symbolic *Portrait*', *The Henry James Review*, vol. 18, no. 2, 1997, pp. 194–6.

Bentley, Nancy. '"Conscious Observation of a Lovely Woman": Jane Campion's *Portrait* in Film', *The Henry James Review*, vol. 18, no. 2, 1997, pp. 174–9.

Bousquet, Marc. 'I Don't Like Isabel Archer', *The Henry James Review*, vol. 18, no. 2, 1997, pp. 197–9.

Chandler, Karen Michele. 'Agency and Constraint in Jane Campion's *The Portrait of a Lady*', *The Henry James Review*, vol. 18, no. 2, 1997, pp. 191–3.

Francke, Lizzie. 'On the Brink', *Sight and Sound*, November 1996, pp. 6–9.

Gentry, Ric. 'Painterly Touches' (interview with Stuart Dryburgh), *American Cinematographer*, vol. 78, no. 1, January 1997, pp. 50–7.

Jones, Laura. *The Portrait of a Lady: Screenplay* (London and New York: Penguin Books, 1996).

Murphy, Kathleen. 'Jane Campion's Shining: Portrait of a Director', *Film Comment*, vol. 2, no. 6, November–December 1996, pp. 28–33.

Nadel, Alan. 'The Search for Cinematic Identity and a Good Man: Jane Campion's Appropriation of James's *Portrait*', *The Henry James Review*, vol. 18, no. 2, 1997, pp. 180–3.

Nicholls, Mark. 'She Who Gets Slapped: Jane Campion's *Portrait of a Lady*', *Metro*, no. 111, 1997, pp. 43–7.

Portrait: Jane Campion and The Portrait of a Lady, documentary film by Peter Long and Kate Ellis, 1996.

Viviani, Christian. 'Portrait de femme: L'art d'un portrait', *Positif*, no. 430, December 1996, pp. 6–8.

Walton, Priscilla. 'Jane and James Go to the Movies: Post-Colonial Portraits of a Lady', *The Henry James Review*, vol. 18, no. 2, 1997, pp. 187–90.

Williams, Sue. 'The Portrait of a Certain Lady' (on the making of the film), *The Weekend Australian*, 7 December 1996, pp. 72–6.

Wright Wexman, Virginia. 'The Portrait of a Body', *The Henry James Review*, vol. 18, no. 2, 1997, pp. 184–6.

Holy Smoke

Campion, Anna and Jane. *Holy Smoke* (New York: Hyperion, 1999).

Campion, Anna. 'Scenes from a Dreamtime Odyssey', *Sunday Herald-Sun*,1st edn, 30 January 2000, p. Z16.

Gillett, Sue. 'Never a Native: Deconstructing Home and Heart in *Holy Smoke*', *Senses of Cinema*, no. 5, April 2000; www.sensesofcinema.com/contents/00/5/holy.html

Lewis, Judith. 'Wholly Jane: Jane Campion on Her New Movie *and* Other Mysteries', *LA Weekly*, January 2000; www.laweekly.com/ink/00/09/film-lewis.shtml

McKew, Maxine. 'Jane Campion and *Holy Smoke*' (interview), *ABC 7:30 Report* (Australia), 13 December 1999 www.abc.net.au/7.30/stories/s73088.htm

Murphy, Kathleen. 'Jane Campion's Passage to India' (essay with interpolated comments by Jane Campion), *Film Comment*, vol. 36, no. 1, January–February 2000, pp. 30–6.

Pullinger, Kate. 'Soul Survivor', *Sight and Sound*, October 1999, pp. 8–11.
Raskin, Sarah. 'Holy Helmer' (interview with Jane Campion), *TNT's Rough Cut*; www.roughcut.com/features/qas/jane_campion.html
The Religious Report, 'A Conversation with Jane Campion', *Radio International* (Australia), 22 December 1999.
Urban, Andrew L. 'Hallucination F/X' (interview with *Holy Smoke*'s digital effects supervisor), *Urban Cinefile*; www.urbancinefile.com.au/print/article_view.asp?Article_ID=2836

FILMOGRAPHY

Tissues

1980
Super-8

Mishaps: Seduction and Conquest

1982
Video

Peel: An Exercise in Discipline

1982
Screenplay: Jane Campion
Photography: Sally Bongers
Editing: Jane Campion
Cast: Tim Pye (Brother/Father), Katie Pye (Sister/Aunt), Ben Martin (Son/Nephew)
Production: Ulla Ryghe
Running Time: 9 minutes – Colour

Passionless Moments

1983
Screenplay: Jane Campion and Gerard Lee
Photography: Jane Campion
Editing: Veronika Haeussler
Cast: David Benton (Ed Turmbury), Ann Burriman (Gwen Gilbert), Sean Callinan (Jim Newbury), Paul Chubb (Jim Simpson), Sue Collie (Angela Elliott), Elias Ibrahim (Ibrahim Ibrahim), Paul Melchert (Arnold), George Nezovic (Gavin Metchalle), Jamie Pride (Lyndsay Aldridge), Yves Stenning (Shaun), Rebecca Stewart (Julie Fry)
Production: Jane Campion
Running Time: 9 minutes – Black and White

A Girl's Own Story

1984
Screenplay: Jane Campion
Photography: Sally Bongers
Editing: Christopher Lancaster
Music: Alex Proyas
Cast: Paul Chubb (Father), Jane Edwards (Deidre), Colleen Fitzpatrick (Mother), Joanne Gabbe (Sister), John Godden (Graeme), Geraldine Haywood (Stella), Marina Knight (Gloria), Gabrielle Shornegg (Pam)
Production: Jane Campion
Running Time: 26 minutes – Black and White

After Hours

1984
Screenplay: Jane Campion
Photography: Laurie McInnes
Editing: Annabelle Sheehan
Music: Alex Proyas
Cast: Danielle Pearse (Lorraine), Anna-Maria Monticelli (Sandra Adams), Don Reid (John Phillips)
Production Company: Woman's Film Unit of Film Australia
Running Time: 27 minutes – Colour

Dancing Daze

1985
Episode of television series
Colour

Two Friends

1986
Screenplay: Helen Garner

Photography: Juliann Penney
Editing: Bill Russo
Music: Martin Armiger
Production Design: Janet Patterson
Costume Design: Janet Patterson
Cast: Kris Bidenko (Kelly), Emma Coles (Louise), Sean Travers (Matthew), Kris McQuade (Louise's mother)
Production: Jan Chapman
Running Time: 76 minutes
Made for TV Film – Colour

Sweetie

1989
Screenplay: Jane Campion and Gerard Lee
Photography: Sally Bongers
Editing: Veronika Haeussler
Music: Martin Armiger
Costume Design: Amanda Lovejoy
Cast: Geneviève Lemon (Dawn, aka Sweetie), Karen Colston (Kay), Tom Lycos (Louis), Jon Darling (Gordon), Dorothy Barry (Flo), Michael Lake (Bob), Andre Pataczek (Clayton)
Production: William MacKinnon and John Maynard
Running Time: 97 minutes – Colour

An Angel at My Table

1990
Screenplay: Laura Jones
Photography: Stuart Dryburgh
Editing: Veronika Haeussler
Music: Don McGlashen
Costume Design: Glenys Jackson
Production Design: Grant Major
Cast: Kerry Fox (Janet Frame), Alexia Keogh (Young Janet), Karen Fergusson (Teenage Janet), Iris Churn (Mother), Kevin J. Wilson (Father), Melina Bernecker (Myrtle), Edith Campion (Miss Lindsay)
Production: Bridget Ikin, Grant Major, John Maynard
Running Time: 157 minutes – Colour

The Piano

1993
Screenplay: Jane Campion
Photography: Stuart Dryburgh
Editing: Veronika Jenet
Sound Design: Lee Smith
Music: Michael Nyman
Production Design: Andrew McAlpine
Costume Design: Janet Patterson
Cast: Holly Hunter (Ada), Harvey Keitel (Baines), Sam Neill (Stewart), Anna Paquin (Flora), Kerry Walker (Aunt Morag), Geneviève Lemon (Nessie)
Production: Jan Chapman, Alain Depardieu, Mark Turnbull
Production Company: CiBy 2000
Running Time: 120 minutes – Colour

The Portrait of a Lady

1996
Screenplay: Laura Jones
Photography: Stuart Dryburgh
Editing: Veronika Jenet
Sound Design: Lee Smith
Music: Wojciech Kilar
Production Design: Janet Patterson
Costume Design: Janet Patterson
Cast: Nicole Kidman (Isabel Archer), John Malkovich (Gilbert Osmond), Barbara Hershey (Madame Serena Merle), Mary-Louise Parker (Henrietta Stackpole), Martin Donovan (Ralph Touchett), Shelley Winters (Mrs Touchett), Richard

E. Grant (Lord Warburton), Shelley Duvall (Countess Gemini), Christian Bale (Edward Rosier), Viggo Mortensen (Caspar Goodwood), Valentina Cervi (Pansy Osmond), John Gielgud (Mr Touchett)
Production: Steve Golin, Monty Montgomery, Ann Wingate, Mark Turnbull, Ute Leonhardt, Hedrun Reshoeft
Production Company: Polygram Filmed Entertainment
Running Time: 144 minutes – Colour

Holy Smoke

1999
Screenplay: Anna Campion and Jane Campion
Photography: Dion Beebe
Editing: Veronika Jenet
Sound Design: Lee Smith
Music: Angelo Badalamenti
Production Design: Janet Patterson
Costume Design: Janet Patterson
Cast: Kate Winslet (Ruth Barron), Harvey Keitel (P. J. Waters), Pam Grier (Carol), Julie Hamilton (Mrs Barron), Sophie Lee (Yvonne), Dan Wyllie (Robbie), Paul Goddard (Tim), Tim Robertson (Mr Barron), George Mangos (Yani)
Production: Jan Chapman, Mark Turnbull, Bob Weinstein, Harvey Weinstein, Julie Goldstein
Production Company: Miramax
Running Time: 114 minutes – Colour

INDEX